To: Henry

G Ruiedo 58

keep winning!

WINNING

FROM WALK-ON TO CAPTAIN
IN FOOTBALL AND LIFE

GARY BRACKETT

CLERISY PRESS

Published by Clerisy Press
Printed in the United States of America
Distributed by Publishers Group West
First edition, second printing
For further information, contact the publisher at:
Clerisy Press
Keen Communications
PO Box 43673
Birmingham, AL 35243

www.clerisypress.com

Library of Congress Cataloging-in-Publication Data is available
from the Library of Congress

ISBN 978-1-57860-519-4

Cover and interior designed by Stephen Sullivan

Photos on pages 11, 13, 14, 16, 23, 34, 64, 116, 126, 143, 180, 187, 190, 193, 202, 208, and
the front and back cover, plus title page are property of the Indianapolis Colts, reprinted with
their permission.

Photos on pages 24, 27, 31, 36, 42, 44, 47, 48, 52, 55, 69, 76, 82, 98, 106, 110, 122, 152,
159, 160, 179, 194 and 200 are photos from Gary Brackett and his family, reprinted with
permission.

Photo on page 56-77 from the Post-Courier, reprinted with permission.

Photo on page 92, Rutgers University, reprinted with permission.

Photo on pages 146, 148, 168, and 184-185, Michael Patton, reprinted with permission.

Photo on page 194, Andrew Scalini, reprinted with permission.

This book is dedicated to my mother and father.
Thanks for always believing in me and teaching me the value
in Proverbs 22:6.

"Train up a child in the way he should go,
and when he is old, he will not depart from it."

ACKNOWLEDGMENTS

First of all I would like to thank my wife, Ragan. You amaze me with your strength. You were able to gracefully bear two beautiful children, Gabrielle and Gary Jr., while being in medical school. I love you,,,

Also, I would like to thank my brothers and sisters, Granville, Greg, Grant, and Gwen, and my two half sisters, Zeanetta and Cassandra. Also, all of my nieces and nephews—there are sixteen of them, so they know who they are. Big Cuz Lew, Gram, Aunt Lori, and all of my family members who supported me though my Journey.

Special thanks to all of my football coaches: Robert Cleary, Herb Neilo, Greg Schiano, Tony Dungy, and Jim Caldwell. Position coaches: Mike Dick, Rod Sharpless, Dave Steckel, Marc D'Onofrio, and Mike Murphy.

To all of the players I played with—especially Abdul Payne, L. J. Smith, Dewayne Thompson, Cato June, and David Thornton—for the many memories and good times on and off the field.

Thanks to my editors, Kevin Anderson and Timothy Alford, for all of the help with organizing my thoughts and ideas and moving forward with this book.

Also to Drew Miroff, my attorney, friend, and confidante, for being a great sounding board and offering insight on my decision.

Thanks to Clerisy Press and Richard Hunt for believing in this book and supporting it so that it could be shared with you.

And last, but certainly not least, thank you to the fans who have supported me over the years, going way back to my Glassboro days, then on to Rutgers, and now as a Colt. Thanks for cheering and believing in me, as well as sending me all of the fan mail, filled with strategy and stories of triumph. Thanks most of all for urging me to write this book and share my story, which I gratefully did, so that this in turn might inspire others. Well, here it is and I sure hope you enjoy it!

FOREWORD

BY TONY DUNGY

When I first got into coaching, Chuck Noll was my boss. He would tell me before I went on scouting trips, "Don't go to the weighing and measuring sessions. And don't take your stopwatch. Just watch the games, and then the films, and see who's making the plays. Those are the guys we want to have on our team."

Gary Brackett is one of those guys you *always* want on your team. But if I had carried a certain standard for an Indianapolis Colts player in terms of height, weight, speed, especially as a middle linebacker, he wouldn't have made it. If you were in a grocery store or at the zoo, you wouldn't walk by Gary Brackett and think, "That guy is the middle linebacker for an NFL team." So to do what he has done is both physically and mentally incredible. He's so competitive and so smart that when those qualities are coupled with his desire to play and win, you, as the coach, want him on the field at game time.

Much has been made of Gary being undrafted by the Colts and becoming, in time, our defensive captain. Sometimes fans think it's harder for coaches to keep a free-agent rookie like Gary over someone they drafted. Actually, it isn't hard at all to keep the players who shine in training camp if your commitment is to be fair to the team and build your success around those who will give you their utmost, and their utmost fits the needs of the team. I always prayed that I didn't let personal feelings sway me when making final decisions. We needed to be objective and fair, to keep those guys who are best for the team.

Gary is one of those guys who *wins* for you. You're going to get a lot done with people like Gary, a guy who makes the players around him perform better. On good teams, those players stand out and get an opportunity because the organization is committed to do what's best overall. For a coach, it's very rewarding to see something special in a player, to believe there's something unique about him, and to know you have the support of everyone associated with the team to choose him regardless of who might have been drafted over him—then to see that person rise to a leadership role on and off the field.

The intangibles that Gary brings to the game make him a standout player—his perseverance and toughness and discipline and commitment to be the best. Yes, he's the exception to the rule...and it's true, you can go broke looking for the exceptions. Gary wouldn't say this, but it's very hard to play in the NFL at his size. Sometimes when you see a picture of him in the huddle, surrounded by all those huge defensive guys, you almost can't believe it. And he's the leader of that group! As captain, he's the individual who all those bigger guys look to and follow. That's when you realize it's the personal qualities that an individual brings to the game that will help your team the most.

What made the biggest impression upon me, right from the start, was Gary's desire. When we first talked to him, he told me about growing up in New Jersey and wanting to play for his home state school, Rutgers, even if they couldn't give him a scholarship. That was a big deal to him; he committed to do whatever it took to make that team. That sort of desire is what separates the almost-make-it players from the truly great ones.

Gary's not an extrovert, and he's certainly not the first guy you'd notice in terms of who's talking. But he plays, and lives, with a lot of emotion. Emotion is a key quality you look for in a player, and even moreso, a leader.

I've always believed that a captain should be elected instead of appointed. By electing someone to be your captain, it signals that this individual was selected by the team to represent the team, so we always voted. Captains were not just a title. David Thornton had been our defensive captain. When he went to Tennessee, I wasn't sure who the team was going to chose to replace him. There were a lot of very good players on that defensive team. Also, Gary hadn't been there for very long and had only been a starter for a year.

Surprisingly, the vote was a landslide. I took this to mean that the team recognized a lot of the same things in Gary that the other coaches and I saw in him. To get 90 percent of the votes meant that as a group, the team knew who they wanted to represent them, as well as recognizing his toughness and ability to handle pressure.

Your captains do a great deal more than most fans think. As the coach, my job was to deliver a winner, but you need everyone to buy into the program. Gary and Peyton Manning did such a great job for us, reinforcing the message that the coaches delivered in the locker room and putting it into action on the field. Captains also serve as representatives of the players off the field. I say that my door is always open, but there are a lot of players, especially the young guys, who don't feel comfortable coming into my office. With Gary as their captain, they knew they had someone they could talk to who would carry their message forward.

In the same way, the coaches knew they could talk to the captains about keeping their fingers on the pulse of the team. When you're in the unfortunate situation of needing to discipline a player for violating a rule, you need to have the captains backing you up to maintain the unity of the team. Sometimes the captains try to keep an eye on a guy if he's having personal problems or emotional issues. It's a vital role they play, and I relied on Gary and Peyton for input, even when things were going well and we were rolling. I'd say that I was thinking about giving the team an extra day off, and they'd say, maybe we could just practice without pads.

There's a different approach you have to take when coaching the pros versus high school or college. First and foremost, you're coaching twenty-two- and thirty-two-year-old guys. You don't want them to see you in the narrow role of ultimate authority. You want to be their leader, not their dictator. In the pros, you're coaching guys with mature thought processes and

lots of experience. You're not instructing them so much as leading them. You have to win their faith in you and in your system.

If the captains are on board, the rest of the team will come around. The captains are bound to be closer to them in a player-to-player relationship. Gary's influence was yet another way he was so valuable to the Colts' success: he helped me get my point across through reinforcement at the peer level. He would show the others that by working hard, doing the basics the right way all the time, this is how we do it in Indy. I know these things sound clichéd from a coach, but when they're communicated by a player, that's how teams win.

Gary was instrumental in pulling our defense together. Frankly, we were just as worried in games when Gary wasn't playing as when Peyton wasn't out there. His absence might not have been as noticeable as Peyton's because he didn't handle the ball, but he was just as important to the defense and to the team.

Fans only get to see the players for three hours on Sunday. I was privileged to get a fuller view of number fifty-eight. I was able to see him interact with teammates all week in practice. I was fortunate to know what he was doing in the community. I was lucky to see the many sides of Gary Brackett that so few fans got to know. That broader perspective made things much richer for me. In fact, the only thing I miss about coaching is seeing guys grow from twenty-two-year-old free agents to thirty-year-old captains. That's what transforms the coach-player relationship in the pros, and that's also what made our teams in Indy so unique and, I believe, so successful.

Gary was exemplary in many ways, on and off the field. I remember when we played Kansas City on Halloween in 2004. We had had a very good year in 2003, but we lost to the Patriots in the championship game. But having made it that far reinforced the belief that we were a great team, if we performed up to our potential, and many people picked us to go all the way the next year.

Well, we lost that game to KC despite scoring 35 points. We knew we had a very good defense even if it didn't show that night. Some players were expecting the coaches to be upset, but to their surprise, we didn't yell. In the locker room when it was over, I told them that we simply needed to play up to our ability and we'd be fine. I remember Gary coming to me afterward and saying, "That's exactly what we needed to hear, Coach." It was important to know that Gary and I were on same page. It was also important to have him later say, "I have confidence in these guys. We'll get it done."

Another unforgettable play by Gary came again in a game we lost. We were playing the Steelers in the 2006 divisional championship. They jumped out to an early lead, but we were fighting back. Late in the fourth quarter, Pittsburgh had stopped us, got the ball back, and they were close to the goal line. It was an almost impossible situation, with everyone on their team just trying to protect the ball and run out the clock. Gary hit Jerome Bettis

head-on and caused a fumble, which we should have run back all the way to win that game. It was so poignant, as Gary essentially willed himself to do whatever it took to win, watching as he led the charge that came so close to winning that game.

Nonetheless, I believe that what I will remember most about Gary Brackett is when we met in my office and he told me, "I need to give my brother a bone marrow transplant." That's when I found out the whole story of his family. Gary made clear to me during our conversation that he could handle all that trauma and that it wasn't going to negatively affect his performance on the field.

Everyone in the Colts' organization was hoping and praying that everything would turn out all right. Gary was committed to overcoming every

obstacle that stood in his way. He knew he had to do this because he was a match, and it was the right thing to do for his family, but he was just as concerned about the team and the effect this might have on them. He told me, "Don't worry about me, Coach. I'll do what I have to do to be ready." Through it all, he was still concerned about his teammates. That's what makes a captain. That's what makes a leader.

Taking care of your family and community is very important to me, and I'm just as proud of those things as I am about what our team accomplished. Establishing priorities about what's truly most important for young men was explained to me first when I was a rookie with the Steelers. Art Rooney, the owner of the team, would sit down with the new players every year and tell them, "You're going to have a lot of fun playing professional football. But don't ever forget that you're also representing this city and this team. You have to understand your status and don't take it for granted." I tried to pass that approach along to all the teams I coached.

It's great to be a Colt, I tell the team. It's a great lifestyle. Don't forget, though, your responsibility off the field as well. Playing well, playing to win on Sunday is important. But there's also the rest of the week when you are a citizen, part of this community.

That's what it's all about—encouraging young people and spending time at high schools, teaching kids about the value of education and helping them deal with their problems. Gary, because of his experiences, has developed an amazing compassion that makes him special. When he shares his story, he knows to talk not only about the wins, but also about the losses.

You have to remind yourself that the pros are just young men, with the emphasis on *young*. There will be, on occasion, tragedies that arise with their parents—they are of that age. But to lose both parents and a brother in such a short time, like Gary did, you have to wonder if someone can persevere through all that. You can't downplay ability, because it's not all intangibles and emotion, and this is a very tough, very physical game; so the player's mind has to be just as strong as his body. Gary's experiences of fighting for a place on the team, at every level, and then fighting through seasons when the team was not winning, those experiences tempered him. Those ordeals helped make him strong enough to face the bigger crises in his personal life.

When you suffer those moments that emotionally take the air out of you, if and how you come back determines how you will fare in life. It's how you come back from the losses of life, not losses of games, that defines you as a team and as person. The Colts suffered many devastating losses off the field, starting in '03 with Gary's family, my son in '05, and Reggie Wayne's brother in '06. These events are not something you prepare for as a coach as you're trying to get your team ready to play on Sunday. Through it all, our team would always come together, drawing closer, getting stronger through this support.

Because of Gary's family experience, his role as captain became even more crucial during those times. To be Gary's age and understand that leading a team with perseverance is more gratifying than any game-winning play is simply incredible. But that's who Gary is—a very brave, tough, thoughtful, and caring man who's destined for even greater things in life.

1

You know how some days you wake up and just feel different? And how the craziest of things can get you going? Well, this was one of those days. The sun seemed to shine a bit brighter through the window. My breakfast tasted a little better. The SportsCenter anchor's jokes were slightly funnier.

It was almost like Christmas morning, except instead of a football or the toys I anxiously awaited as a child, on this day I awaited something…a bit different. The doorbell rang. A FedEx van pulled away as I reached the front door, where an Astor & Black box sat. This could only be one thing. I knew it was my suit. This was going to be clean, I tell you. Clean! Clean is the only word that works when things are this perfect. I'm gonna be cleaner than the Board of Health. To go with this perfect suit, I found the exact pair of socks I needed. Purple socks for a gray suit with purple pinstripes. What could be cleaner than that?

The buzz of a text message snapped me back to reality.

"What time we leavin'?"

I responded right back: "Same."

Since everything was going right, change would be foolish—I intended to ride this wave all the way. He wanted later, I wanted earlier. We had met in the middle and agreed on 1:00. I always wanted to be on time, but he liked to cut it close. Other than that, my boy Cato and I were cut from the same cloth. Since we worked together and lived right next to each other, carpooling made a lot of sense—even more sense in the winter. After a three-hour plane ride, nothing would stink more than digging a car out of February snow all alone.

I walked over to Cato's house, hurdling across the stepping-stones to avoid the snow. The cold invigorated me; the day kept getting better. Cato was decked out in a fine tan suit with an orange liner and orange stripes. He hadn't stopped there: even his shoes were orange.

"You went all out, huh, Cato?"

He laughed, "A man's got to coordinate…got to coordinate! Like I say, unison makes you look good, feel good, and play good."

Normally in the NFL, players order suits to wear as they travel. I usually ordered around six a year and recycled a couple from the previous season. But for the Super Bowl, we took everything up a notch. Just like a businessman who wants to look his best for big deals, football players want to look especially good for big games. So, many players get suits specially tailored for them in preparation for the biggest game. The tailor already has your measurements from throughout the year, so you select the colors or cut, tell them about any extras you want added, put in the rush order, and wait anxiously. Well, that is what Cato and I did, and the results were definitely worth the wait!

As we stood together laughing over our fits, particularly fine suits for this day, Cato asked, "How you feelin', G Baby?"

He always referred to me as G Baby, one of my many nicknames in many circles.

"Good, man, good," I replied.

"When's your fam heading down?"

"Prob next week."

"Who's coming with? Mom and dad? Brothers and sisters?"

And just like that, the morning's good mood dropped a few degrees as Cato realized his misstep.

"No, man, just the brothers and sister."

"Aw, my bad. That's what I meant."

I didn't blame him. People shouldn't have to tiptoe around my parents' passing. After all, no one expects someone this young to be in my situation. Of the many challenges I've faced, this one continues to shake me: life's highs just aren't the same without my parents. But, every person, even those who might be considered "average" faces extraordinary challenges. We are all forged and fueled by fires. I don't believe we can ever prevent them, so the crucial question is how well we will handle them? Will we burn away, or will we develop resilience for future fights? Will we shrink or grow? I say grow. Fight or take flight? I guess I was always one to choose fight.

Cato and I came up together in the league. In 2003, he was a sixth-round draft pick out of Michigan and I was an undrafted rookie free agent, which meant that during tryouts—I still remember the anxiety—we had plenty of reasons to worry about whether or not we would make the squad.

We have shared, and still share, many common experiences. As the big money earners in our families, we both feel responsible for others in a way we didn't experience until making the NFL. We both know what it's like to have others look to you for help. We also share the common drive to be the most-prepared player each and every day we step on the field. Whereas most players watch game film on DVD players, Cato and I both bring computers, like the coaches, to review and dissect film more thoroughly. These computers allow the player to pause, rewind in slow motion, and edit out sequences to highlight common tendencies or weaknesses. After all this film work, we always compare notes and try to anticipate what our opposition is going to do.

Football players have all sorts of time commitments, many of which are common to the whole team. So, in addition to our shared focus on film, we decided to share a neighborhood. We bought houses together and decided that we would be permanent carpool mates.

Now we were leaving together for the biggest moment of our professional careers. We left for the Colts' facility, where we would board a team bus that would take us to the airport. After that...Miami!

In our excitement, we talked plays as we drove to our destination. We focused particularly on the Chicago's NFC Championship game against the New Orleans Saints. We analyzed their tendencies, strengths, and weaknesses. We also talked some of our recent victory in the AFC Championship game over the New England Patriots. We'd won on a great second-half comeback; the W had been sealed by an interception in the final minutes. However, our excitement over that victory paled in comparison to the opportunity granted to us as a result. Beating the Pats put us in the biggest game of our life, the Super Bowl.

Team flights always leave at 2:00 p.m. Waiting for us when we arrived at the Colts' facility was a nice surprise. They were letting the players park on the practice turf in the barn. An assistant equipment manager directed us to our spot.

"You guys can pull over there by Dwight Freeney, Mr. Brackett."

"Man, I can't believe you're letting us park inside."

"Well Gary, you know they are forecasting a big February storm. We didn't want the Super Bowl champs to come back and have to dig their cars out!"

"Super Bowl champs, huh? That has a nice ring to it. We'll see what we can do."

"All right, after you park, check on your tickets, tag your bags, and make sure everything is in order."

As we climbed out of the car, Cato and I noticed that we weren't the only guys who were all decked out. The southern guys wore grills that sparkled golden when they smiled. Diamond chains surrounded most players' necks—the rookies were getting a bit of grief for theirs. Since we knew their salaries, and knew how much we had paid for our own chains, it was pretty simple to do the math on the fly. Any chain a rookie wore that was larger than ours—especially if it was three times larger—had to be fake! As I looked at the fake attempts at style I couldn't help but ask a young practice squad player (fully expecting a lie), "How much did you pay for that chain?"

"Couple bucks."

"My leg…"

"What about your leg?"

"You're pullin' it."

The chain probably wasn't worth more than a few hundred or so. There was no way he could afford a diamond chain like that as a rookie.

Dominic Rhodes, our fearless and personable running back, couldn't resist greeting the rooks with some jabs, "Hey, hey, where did you get that suit?

Burlington Coat Factory? Target?"

"No chance, bro."

The most cutting insult for a guy dressed in a tailored suit was to ask if he just got it off the rack at some store.

"Yeah, Dominic, well at least I didn't steal my shoes from Ronald Mc-Donald! Where'd you get those clown boots anyway?"

Even though we were throwing jabs, it was all fun and games. Sometimes in life you have to pat yourself on the back. Sometimes you have to throw a personal party, send flowers to yourself, and go out and buy yourself something nice. We were going to the Super Bowl and were dressed for success. My philosophy has always been: make an investment in yourself. Well, I had invested in myself for so long. I'd spent so many days on the practice field, in the weight room, and choosing the healthier options in the cafeteria over the more enticing ones. We have most certainly invested in ourselves to get here. Why not have a bit of fun along the way?

As we got on the bus, guys followed the unwritten seating assignments: veterans in the front—another tangible reward for their years of service. Seats up front meant being first to board the plane, first to get food, and, of course, respect. Veterans lead the team on the bus and plane, just as they lead on the field.

We all noticed the new plane that our bus pulled up to. It looked like Mr. Irsay, the owner of the team, had pulled out all the stops. Reggie Wayne took a seat up front, and I sat next to him. Mathis was across from Cato in the next row.

When we arrived in Miami, the team would relax for the evening before the next day's activities—meetings about coverages, schemes, and game planning to brush up on. No one complained about the schedule. This was uncharted territory for us, and we definitely wanted to take advantage of a golden opportunity.

Usually, these kinds of trips weren't much more than a business trip, but guys wanted to document this particular experience. Despite our awareness of this trip's serious nature, we felt like a bunch of school kids as we boarded the plane. Fancy cameras and camcorders were out. My dad once said, "The only difference between men and boys is the price of their toys." Well, Dad would have felt himself vindicated if he'd seen this plane's company. Everyone was wearing the latest watches and fresh suits, chains, and fronts. All the excitement was fine, but we had to make sure we didn't get distracted from our main goal by getting caught up in all the glitz and glamour of South Beach. We had business to accomplish: winning a world championship and bringing home the Vince Lombardi Trophy.

As soon as we took off, some guys started rolling dice and playing booray. Some guys look at the Super Bowl bonuses as play money—unexpected income. Guys had anywhere from $10,000 to $20,000 on hand and were expecting to win or lose big. Card games were always rich on NFL flights, and this one was gonna be richer than others. I don't usually play. I'm more of a spades player, myself.

Rookies were required to bring food for the veterans. What will it be for my snack today? KFC? Subway? Buffalo Wild Wings? Something else? I settle for some wings from BW3s, courtesy of Freddy Keiaho.

· · · · ·

As I finally reached my seat, well-fed and excited about the coming week, I felt the urge to play some music on my computer. When I opened up my Mac Book Pro and turned on some Jay-Z, I noticed that I had forgotten to load my pictures from the AFC Championship game. I had a limited amount of space left on my memory stick, so I began to upload pictures from my camera to my computer. The pictures finished loading, and I began to look though some of them. The way iPhoto works, the oldest photo comes up on the top—some old pictures my sister had sent a while back popped up first on screen. I hesitated for a moment as the picture triggered an old feeling. My family and I are standing in front of our house in Glassboro, New Jersey—must be about 1984, because I look like I'm around four or five years old. Milestones and achievements stir reflection, and I couldn't help but tie that memory to this new one I was now making. Wow, the picture looks to be so old, and at the same time it feels like just yesterday....

The picture I looked at first has been the source of countless jokes over the years. It depicts all of my immediate family gathered together at our house. For some reason, we are sporting nametags. Perhaps this was a neighborhood function or family reunion. Though the exact memory has faded, the feeling of those days remains. I look at the picture and can almost hear the sounds, can feel the warmth of the day, not quite hot, but warm.

Our mother had arranged us in descending order from oldest to youngest. Granville stands on the far left and is bored and uninterested in the photographer. To his left stands Greg. He has worn a striped tank top identical to Granville's. I don't view this imitation with negative judgment. The younger brothers all admired and copied the older ones. Nothing wrong with being a copycat as long as you're copying the right cat! Apparently, Grant and I had decided it was too warm for full shirts, even tank tops, and instead we chose for the day our standard '80s half shirt. Behind us, tucked under our father's big legs, huddled the youngest, and our only sister, Gwendolyn.

We kids were uninterested in the task at hand, and a close look at the photo reveals less about our personalities than our boredom. But if you look closely at my parents, you can tell certain things about their life and times. Mom had a rather unfortunate Jheri curl. She smiles slightly, the smile of someone who understands the difficulties of daily living, yet is happy to have her family around her. Her stance is revealing. She does not stand haughty or proud, but solid. She was in many ways our rock. Dad's gestures are just as telling. He is shouting in the direction of someone outside the frame. His head is arched back and in one hand he is holding a frosty mug, just emptied, not yet filled with a new beer. Perhaps the most noticeable thing about him is his size. He is broad shouldered and tall. He looks fit. He does not stand like someone who should be trifled with. And that was him. A former Marine, he took life seriously and always demanded that we be places punctually. At the same time, he also wasn't afraid to cut loose a bit with a drink or two.

The photo was taken in Glassboro, New Jersey, where we had just moved from Camden. For those who are unfamiliar with the statistics of crime throughout the country, Camden often takes the dubious prize of Most Dangerous City in America. This statistic is based on numbers compiled by the FBI regarding the number of violent crimes per person. Some of Camden's citizens wear this ranking with pride, with T-shirts that say on the front *# 1 in America* (and on the back) *America's Worst City.*

Situated just across the river from of the City of Brotherly Love, Philadelphia, many parts of Camden, New Jersey, are noticeably unbrotherly. Perhaps many of the problems are the result of poverty. Two out of five citizens live below the poverty line, and the school system was recently taken over by the state of New Jersey due to student drop-out rates.

Behind us in the photo sits our new home. With four bedrooms and two bathrooms, it was a great improvement over our previous living situation. If the first photo on my computer had been of our home in Camden, it would have pictured a row home with three bedrooms and a bathroom that was perpetually broken. Many houses on our row, these were the row houses you hear frequently about in discussions of American crime, were boarded up. Other neighboring houses in Camden suggested a complete lack of civic pride, or perhaps just patchwork ingenuity. From the wide array of building materials, it was clear that when something broke, whatever was cheapest would serve as a replacement. This fix-it fast, fix-it cheap approach created a hodgepodge of architecture. Brick portions of the house ran straight into faux brick shingle material, as if the builder ran out of money mid-way through construction and chose instead

a less costly option. Cheap siding of multiple types, asbestos shingles, rotting wood, and even portions of tin, "decorated" the fronts of houses and lent a confused look that bespoke poverty. Paint schemes on houses had only one common characteristic—a complete lack of schematic planning and years of age and disuse. The exceptions to the rule, folks bravely holding on to their pride and often defending their homes forcefully, were stuck next to neighbors that neither cared about nor were capable of maintaining appearances. When you account for all the citizens of Camden addicted to drugs of various degrees of illegality, you understand how and why the street came to look the way it did.

The backyard of our Camden house was about the size of a standard jail cell and had a comparable lack of comfort. No lawn, no bushes, just a ten-foot-by-ten-foot section of concrete, just enough room for a picnic table. To many people this lack of a backyard might be a good thing—no grass to cut. But with four boys, it was my mother's nightmare. The lack of space left us with only one option. We had to take our games out into the street up front, dodging cars and drug dealers as we caught passes and ran routes. The most

astounding thing to me now is that on that broken and pothole-riddled as-
phalt, we played tackle. In Camden, toughness developed at a young age. I
still have a scar from tackling Greg in the street and catching a piece of glass
in my leg. When I finally dragged him down, blood streamed from my knee,
tears welled up in the corners of my eyes. Greg carried me inside to get me
cleaned up. Even as he sympathetically helped me bandage the wound, he
looked at me with stern eyes and said in a clear voice, "You gonna have to be
tougher around here to make it, Gary. You can't go crying about little stuff
like this. I know it hurts, but even when you don't think you can bear it...you
can. Just reach down for something extra."

This combination was normal for my brother Greg. He was always caring but firm with me. He had my back, but also insisted that I learn to take up
for myself. He helped teach me that valuable lesson about the size of the dog
in the fight mattering much less than the size of the fight in the dog. This dog
developed particular toughness from playing against older kids early in life,
and from words like these from my brothers. I knew as the smallest kid out
there that I had to make up for what I lacked somehow. Nobody felt sorry for
me, so I had better not feel sorry for myself. This all helped me in the long
run. No one gets better from playing against weaker competition. Challenge
and adversity stir growth!

One episode is seared into my mind. My brothers and I were out in front
of our house in the street. We were playing a game of some sort with neighborhood guys, and for some reason Granville ended up in a tussle with two neighborhood thugs. Without thinking, every one of the Brackett brothers jumped
on those poor guys. They ran off knowing that when you messed with one of
us, you had better expect us all to join, even little me at five years old.

Granville got into another fight that was even more dangerous. On this
day I was near the front door when the altercation broke out. I copied what
I had seen on TV, went inside and grabbed one of my father's handguns and
came out of the house shouting. I had no intention of shooting anything, but
that did nothing to soften the whipping I got when Dad got home and heard
the story.

"This thing is not a toy, Gary! You have no idea the kind of pain you can cause with this gun."

"But, Dad, I wasn't going to use it."

"One thing I always say about guns, Gary, is never get one out and point it at something unless you are prepared to go all the way."

When I was five, my parents decided to move the family to Glassboro, a safer area with more space, and where perhaps we would do a better job of staying out of trouble. Camden's streets were just too dangerous. Our new home was only about twenty minutes away so my older siblings weren't going too far from their friends. But it was some distance into the suburbs and away from the big city of Philly next door. We all helped pack, and as we prepared for the big day I grew nervous and lashed out.

"Mom, what our new house be like?"

"You'll like it, Gary. We'll have more of a yard to play in."

"Yeah, but what about my old room? What about my friends?"

"You will have an even bigger room, and across the street you and your brothers will be able to make forts!"

"Mom, I don't want to go!"

"Gary, you remember what I always tell you now: don't fear and don't be angry. One minute of anger robs you of sixty seconds of happiness."

As a young kid I had no reason to doubt my mom. She never led me wrong. But I had heard her and dad whispering late at night about the move. They knew it needed to happen, but moving five kids even a short distance is a chore.

In Glassboro, things were definitely better. The schools were friendlier places with fewer students and nicer teachers. Our new house had more room, another bedroom and bathroom to be exact. We thought we had gone to heaven. There was more than one bathroom, and both of them were functional. Even more exciting than the new space inside the house was the new space outside. No more playing in the street and getting glass in our knees. We now had a yard!

The front of the house emptied out into the projects. We lived right across from a federal government housing development, each of the little brick houses was essentially the same design. But in between those projects and our house grew grass. And our backyard stretched back perhaps a half football field into some woods. The side yard extended for about fifty yards before it sloped gently into a drainage ditch. We played football and baseball year-round. And here is the best part of growing up with four boys in a house: no need to recruit because you always have numbers for a game of two on two. We Bracketts had enough to field a game with just the brothers. Since I was the youngest, and Greg was the second oldest, we often ended up playing against Granville and Grant. Greg and I developed our own secret language for plays, used hand signals our brothers never could decipher, and were usually encouraging teammates.

This neighborhood was a more family-friendly place. Sometimes at night we would play late, and Dad would come outside and whistle. That whistle covered the whole projects, and reached clearly to the basketball courts where we so often spent our time. If we didn't hear it, others did. Those who lived around us knew two things: if that whistle sounded, Granville Brackett expected his boys home. And he didn't expect them sooner or later, he expected them to be there quick! Not now, but RIGHT now. So, that whistle was our family version of: "ThunderCats ThunderCats ThunderCats Ho!" At that sound, we dropped what we were doing, ended whatever game we were playing, and moved.

If we weren't playing sports, we went around gathering up cardboard from curbs and dumpsters, using it to construct forts in the vacant lot across from our house. In these forts we pretended we were trapped in a forest and surrounded on all sides by enemies. We envisioned ourselves in foreign lands. But when it rained, we were right back in New Jersey and faced a problem our neighbors here in Glassboro struggled with: we were evicted. Was everything perfect in Glassboro? Not by a long shot. But things were better than Camden. And after all, we are always involved in accepting our own perceptions and realities. Sometimes we had to sell ourselves on the idea of our own life. Even though we knew it might rain, we still built the forts. And while

those protective cardboard homes were still standing, we had some fun in them. Often, we must make and shape our own reality.

Ever since I can remember, I knew without a doubt that I wanted my reality to involve football. When I told people this around middle school they surely thought: who doesn't? My attraction to the sport was borne out of a particular experience. In the seventh grade, the one and only Reggie White came to visit our school. He played for the beloved Philadelphia Eagles and was my favorite player. The day of his visit, the place buzzed with excitement.

"Reggie White is gonna be here."

"Gary, you think he'll sign autographs?"

"I don't care about autographs. I just want to see how big he is!"

When Reggie spoke in the auditorium, he talked about why other players and coaches referred to him as "the minister of defense." He talked about dreaming big and reaching for the clouds, because even if you miss you'll be among the stars. When we kids looked up at Reggie, we thought that he probably didn't have to reach too far for those stars. He was absolutely massive! But after hearing that speech I dreamed big. Our class talked about it afterwards and the teacher asked, "Gary, what do you want to do with your life?"

"I want to play in the NFL."

The teacher grimaced subtly, "What *else* might you want to do?"

I did not budge or offer an alternative, but I also did not say what I thought next. I thought it might be disrespectful and get me in trouble. My mind burned with a singular thought: *I will play in the NFL some day.*

Too often in today's world kids don't know or care what they want to do with their lives. When I ask children today the questions my teacher posed to me, the kids who say "nothing" really scare me. Those kids will be the ones who get exactly what they planned for: *Nothing*! After all, people don't usually plan to fail, but too often they fail to plan. No one wants to live check to check for most of his or her life. But many people do. In my opinion, your perspective on life often determines the amount of success you have in it. From early on, I set goals and worked methodically to achieve them. Sure there were roadblocks along the way and points where I strayed from the path, but I never forgot the path I was seeking and always hustled back to it.

I was taught these values, in large part, through the examples set for me by older brothers. As I started playing more sports, my reality began to revolve increasingly around my brothers Granville, Greg, and Grant. Each of them was athletically talented. Each played three sports in high school. Granville, the oldest, probably looked at us, his younger brothers, with a bit of annoyance. After all, his primary perception of us was as kids he had to baby-sit. Grant was closest to my own age, and so we were on many teams together. We had a unique bond due to this proximity in years. Like many siblings close in age, we competed against each other more than the others.

I looked up to Greg in particular because he played football. He was the stud running back who scored all the touchdowns. When he played defense, he made all the tackles. He was the kid others in high school wanted to be. He was magnetic. Every moment I spent with him, I felt like I was being given a gift. He was a popular kid, a bit more outgoing than the other brothers. We were all captains of our teams, but he was one of the guys who the coaches picked to captain as soon as they could. He had a powerful leadership quality. I remember asking him one day about how he got to be captain.

"Don't lead by talking Gary. Words are meaningless without action. Knowledge doesn't matter nearly as much as people say either. What are you going to do with information? You have to act on it! That's what matters."

Greg lived by those words. He was always the first one in the weight room at practice, pushed others in sprints, and volunteered for the toughest match-ups in basketball. He didn't just talk the talk. He walked the walk in such a way that people wanted to follow him.

"Yo G Baby what you lookin' at?"

My boy Cato brought me back to the present, "Just these old photos. Heading down to this big event, and thinking about some of the folks that got me to this point."

"Yeah, it's wild the folks who helped us get here."

"Man, thinking about my brother Greg. He basically taught me how to play football."

Cato teased me, "I thought you were a man...self-made!"

· · · · ·

"Nah, nah, I ain't self-made. To say that would be a lie and would disrespect everyone who helped get me to this seat on the plane. Without them, there is no way I'd be here. Sometimes you have to believe in someone else's belief in you before your own belief kicks in."

As Cato and I talked, photos from the AFC Championship came up on the screen. Cato looked at one of him and me holding the Lamar Hunt trophy, saying, "Unreal, huh? Coming back and beating them... I thought for sure they had our number somehow," said Cato.

"Yeah," I responded, "Feels even more special since we came back, but still lost those years before. Reminds me of something my father used to say, 'If the mountain was smooth you wouldn't be able to climb it.'"

"Well, G Baby, we got one more to climb this year."

"Yeah, but it feels good to get past that particular peak."

Dad often talked about the difficulties that plague us in life. Even though the rough patches on life's mountain feel like obstacles, they give it shape and actually make the slopes possible to climb. The ability to overcome difficulties was something that Dad demanded, and something with which he had personal experience. From the time we were young, he required us to give effort rather than excuses. One thing he often said, "Gary, son, there is no such thing as a try."

To demonstrate this fact when we were young, he would take a piece of paper in his hand, hold it out a bit beyond my wingspan, and say

"Try to grab it."

Even though I knew what was coming, I'd reach eagerly. As soon as my hand was close, he snatched it away.

"See what I mean? Did you grab the paper?"

"No, sir."

"All right, let's try again."

This time, he'd be a bit slower and I'd succeed.

"What did you just do?"

"I grabbed it, Dad!"

"That's right, son. You grabbed it. Just remember. There's no such thing as a try in life. Either you do something or you don't. Don't lean on tries."

Dad knew all too well about reaching for things, as well as the costs of failing to reach to them. He probably knew well, though he didn't often say this to his sons, that sometimes effort isn't all that is required. He didn't talk much about Vietnam. But his actions suggested a man haunted by his dreams, and sometimes in his waking hours, by things he had seen. Many veterans talk of the dumb luck of survival. To survive a war while your friends die alongside you is perhaps the cruelest form of luck. Movies and books have documented the horrors of the Vietnam War: the psychological torture of sleeping wet, covered in leeches, and fully aware that tomorrow could be your last day. It was a dirty and personal war where death loomed daily as a soldier's most likely fate. Dad came home physically whole...but emotionally broken.

Officially diagnosed with schizophrenia and post-traumatic stress disorder (PTSD), Dad could be fine one minute and absolutely gone the next. People with those illnesses have a hard time distinguishing fiction from reality. For Dad, night was a particular enemy. He slept with one eye open, still not convinced even in the safety of his home that the world was at peace.

His constant vigilance—some would say paranoia—was one mode of protection. But he also had a rifle under the bed, loaded and ready. On the Fourth of July, when everyone else was enjoying the fireworks, Dad was already on edge and near that rifle. If we woke to the sound of sirens, we knew that if we went into the kitchen to get a glass of water, Dad would most likely be there with that rifle, sitting quietly at the table and staring off into the distance.

Sometimes, things grew a bit more violent. One night it was storming and Dad heard the drainpipe, which must have come loose during the previous winter, banging against the side of the house. As he reached the door, the wind picked up and the banging sound accelerated. Relying on instincts from a much darker time, he reacted swiftly, firing his gun at the first thing he saw that moved. Everyone in our house, plus some of the next-door neighbors, awoke to a deafening BOOM! The rattling stopped, and lights from our neighbors' houses came on. When they emerged in pajamas sleepy-eyed, they found the front drainpipe lying on the ground, completely detached from the gutter by the force of the shotgun's shell.

The danger that beleaguered Dad, which he introduced into our lives with his fearful outbursts, occasionally entered our lives even more directly. His ability, at times, to be a loving father suffered gravely due to his PTSD. Every parent eventually loses his or her patience with his or her kids. When a combat-trained Marine happens to do so, and when that loss of patience prompts a full-fledged flashback, things could get genuinely scary.

One such instance was particularly memorable. Our family went to church every Sunday, and generally Dad was in charge of rousing us from bed. On this Sunday, we dreaded going to church just as much as we hated being the only kids there. Every Sunday we protested, and every Sunday we lost the small battle to watch our morning cartoons. Instead, we got church. Grant and I were in a room across the hall, and we had an easier time waking than our elder brothers. On this morning, Greg was particularly sluggish.

Dad's routine was to start with yelling down the stairs, "You all better be up and dressed when I get down there." After this came another level of warning, where Dad knocked on our doors and occasionally came and pulled at our feet to wake us. After that last warning, Dad went upstairs to get dressed himself. On this particular morning, when Dad came back downstairs to the kitchen and found Greg wasn't there, his anger rose. We had been whipped before, so we knew what was coming. Dad entered the room and stood above Greg. He raised his arm and prepared to bring it down hard as he shouted, "I told you to get up!" With the first blow, Greg flinched and picked up his feet. He kicked instinctively to protect himself; his legs somehow connected with Dad's face. With that contact, something snapped. Grant and I stood and watched, horror-stricken for our brother, as Dad climbed on top of him in the bed. Neglecting his usual belt, with closed fists he rained down blow after blow. He hit him everywhere, but most of the punches connected with Greg's chest and face. The screams that came from both of them were terrible and animalistic. Greg pleaded for someone to help him, but the entire family stood watching, helpless. Dad screamed things we did not understand, and he seemed nothing less than possessed.

Time during these kinds of traumatic moments moves differently, but the entire sequence seemed to have lasted about five minutes. It stopped as quickly as it began. Whether because he was tired or because he came back to reality, Dad suddenly stopped hitting Greg and then backed away from the bed. He took two deep breaths, looked around at all of us, went straight to the telephone and dialed 911.

"I need you to come here fast. I just had an out-of-body experience and have severely hurt my son."

The police arrived quickly. After talking with Dad, they came back to the room to talk to Greg. He was in his boxers and told them to come back in a second after he was dressed. We were on the first floor of a two-story house and Greg leapt out the window, not to return for a couple weeks. That night, my other siblings and I heard something unusual coming from our parents' bedroom. Mom tolerated Dad's style of punishment, but after this episode, she drew a hard and fast line. She sided with Greg, her child. We heard them yelling as we lay in bed.

"What are you thinking? Have you gone crazy?"

"I don't know. Something snapped. I felt like I wasn't here anymore, that I was back in a foxhole fighting hand to hand."

She may have been sympathetic to the illness that drove him to violence, but she demanded change,

"You are going to get help! I am not dealing with this anymore. Your pride has kept you from going to see a doctor, but if you want to keep this family together you are leaving here tomorrow morning and not coming back until you deal with this."

I'd almost forgotten about the fight when I woke up the next morning, but there was a feeling in the house that something was just different. I didn't smell the coffee brewing—Dad was the only one who drank it and so he made it— and the paper was still on the front doorstep. As I put together those puzzle pieces, I knew that I hadn't dreamed Mom and Dad's conversation. He was gone.

You deal with this! How were we kids supposed to interpret our father's absence that next morning with those words ringing in our ears? We didn't see him for months, and we wondered if he'd be gone forever.

For kids in the projects, there were two reasons that fathers disappeared: drugs and alcohol. Two-parent households go to single-parent really quick with one long bender strung out on drugs. Even friends would joke about the worst:

"Where's your dad, man?"

"Shut up, I said."

"Dude, you know what they say about getting strung out in those Camden alleys."

When your father disappears after beating your brother so severely, and no explanation is offered, you really don't have much to say in reply to such teasing. At night, we often asked Mom, "Where is Dad? When is he coming home?"

I don't remember how she answered those questions, just that she essentially dodged them. How she must have been wondering the same thing. Hoping just like us for his return. She stayed solid, and though she didn't answer these questions to which she did not know the answer, she did continually say, "Everything is going to be just fine. Don't you all worry about it."

After a couple of months, my mother received a letter in the mail. We were waiting for her to take us somewhere as the mail arrived, and so we watched as she opened this envelop with Dad's handwriting on the front. Her face was awash in emotions, some seemingly in conflict with each other. She shed a single tear, and we knew something really weird was going on. We never saw Mom cry. In addition to being more than a bit confused, I was just excited to see proof that Dad was still alive. Later, we snuck into my parents' room to read the letter, still sitting on her dresser. It was from my father, who seemed to be in good spirits. The letter said he had checked into the Veterans Hospital in Martinsburg, West Virginia. He wrote that he loved her and was sorry to have put her in this position all alone with five kids, but that he had to get his mind right. How must Mom have felt when reading this letter? Happy to know that the love of her life was getting better? Surely. But also, she must have felt some bitterness being left alone with all of us. Whatever anger or frustration she felt, she never let us see it. Dad stayed in the hospital for over two years getting treatments for his PTSD. When we first visited, a couple months after the letter's arrival, a doctor tried to explain to us what Dad was going through.

"This disease changes your Dad's body's response to stress. See, our brain tells our body when it should be scared through chemicals that act like signals in our nerves. People who have been through really stressful things, like war, can get those signals mixed up. He has normal responses that are based on an abnormal past. People with this disease think they are back in war when really they are just in the house. That is why he gets so scary sometimes. Because he thinks he has to be."

As much as the doctor tried to explain things, and he may have done a great job, for an eleven-year-old kid the situation was baffling and frustrating. At that age, you think people get help because they are sick physically. Mental illness just does not make any sense.

In response to the jokes of my peers, I struggled and internally agreed with them at times. People are either crazy or regular, what does that make him? He should be here! He should be at my games.

Now that I'm older, I realize that people usually don't get help because they are weak, but rather because they want to remain strong. The hospital greatly helped my father; he quit smoking and drinking and became a devout Christian. He was eventually given awards at church for his consistent presence and service as an elder and usher. At home, he was less erratic and more able to control his emotions.

These negative experiences were not all of the man as a father, and after his time in the hospital, Dad's positives became more evident. Though he never finished high school, he plugged away until he earned his GED. One of the brightest men I knew, he had his PhD in the streets. He was always aware of things around him, and for many neighbors he served as a kind of porch counselor. He sat there in a chair offering opinions, solicited or not, to any who would listen. For some people he was a trusted bank who held on to their checks, a kind of insurance policy against unwise spending. He advised others about legal rights and taxes. He was perhaps most valuable to

his fellow veterans and was passionate about getting adequate medical attention for PTSD.

That porch was like a microcosm of the projects, and Dad often joked that he didn't need TV. "This porch is like a big screen view of everything you need. I don't need cable. You want fights? Take a look over there to the left. A little inappropriate romance? Look at those two over there. Drugs and violence? All you need is right here from this vantage point."

If he wasn't sitting on that porch, he was cooking on his grill. One of Dad's more lighthearted but avid rules: don't anyone touch my grill! On holidays he could barely sleep for all his excitement about getting up and getting things going. Often Mom teased him affectionately about finishing his cooking before the guests even arrived. He was punctual about every obligation, a value that continues to serve me well and save me money. After all, a tardy arrival to any NFL meeting or any film session can literally cost thousands.

The affection and gratitude I feel today is a new development. As a young boy, I didn't understand his methods. Often I was flustered by Dad's responses to me after games. I'd come home excited,

"You see that, Dad? Two touchdowns and twelve tackles! Did you see? Did ya?"

"Gary, I saw those two missed tackles and that fumble of yours that gave the other team good field position."

I was upset that he wouldn't validate my achievements, but I knew he was proud of me. I had overheard him gushing on the phone with his friends, "You ought to see Gary. Can't nobody stop him, man. That boy of mine has got heart and talent!"

• • • • •

At that age I had a difficult time understanding the contradiction of his words to me and his words about me. The words to me stung, and stayed with me longer. There was ample balm to that sting, though. Our home was not an unloving one, a fact largely due to Mom's influence.

While Dad was always opinionated and often critical, Mom was a source of quiet, steadfast love. Dad always felt somewhat distant. Even the way he looked at us felt removed. With her kids, Mom was as tight as they come. We all knew that Sandra Eileen Brackett was our number-one cheerleader. No matter what other obligations she had, no matter the weather or time, she was always there for us. Someone once told me that we grow into what we see. And what we saw from Mom was a great example of kind, caring, tireless parenthood.

I never really appreciated everything my mother went through and the sacrifices she made so that her children could be successful. When my father was home and we wanted to go out or over to a friend's house, we would ask my father. He did what many men do and told us, "Wait until your mom gets home."

I took Dad at his word. When she would pull up in the driveway, I would run outside the house and before she could get out of the car, I'd exclaim, "Mom, can I..." No offers of help with the bags. No questions about her day. No, "happy to see ya, Mom." And her response was always, "Baby, just give me a minute." I never understood what the minute signified until I began working a full day's work and would arrive home to a chorus of requests when all I wanted was a minute to breathe. Even in the face of sometimes self-absorbed children, Mom never said a bad word about anyone. She often urged us away from the sheer idea of negativity, "If you don't have anything good to say about somebody, don't say anything at all." I wish I had that same quality.

After Dad's episode with Greg and subsequent hospitalization in 1991, things became increasingly tight financially. After all, our household incomes went from two to one. Usually Mom stretched the food to feed everyone. But there were rough weeks when she would glance around the table at the scant portions, and decide to scarf ice instead of eating...all so we could have more. She was so convincing in her decisions: "I'm not hungry tonight. I have no idea where my appetite went. Ya'll split my share!"

On a daily basis, she was someone whose actions did the speaking. In spite of working full-time at two jobs and raising five kids on her own while our father was in treatment, her spirits and love never flagged or waned. Not only was she always in the stands at her kids' games, she was also the mother who organized all the other fans and brought cowbells to ring for celebratory moments.

Mom's most epic scheduling miracle in my eyes took place on opening day of little league baseball. The league had scheduled all of the Brackett children's games to start around the same time. My sister was playing softball; Grant and I were on the Elite Bakery team together; and my brothers Granville and Greg played on Atlantic Electric. Somehow Mom worked her way between all three fields and was there to see every one of our at-bats! She was even able to talk about it on the car ride home.

"How did you watch me, Grant, Greg, Granville, and Gwen, Mom? You only have two eyes!"

"Oh...a mother's magic is a powerful thing, honey."

By watching our activities, Mom supported our interests. But she insisted that we get involved in her interests too. And her interests almost always revolved around church. As a result, we were often there every day of the week. Revival one night, Bible study the next, adult choir on Fridays, and children's choir on Saturdays. All of this was, on a practical level, leading up to Sunday at church. But the most important part for Mom was to have us in

a place where we were safe and exposed to good influences. On a practical level, this constant churchgoing fit her most motherly instinct to be with her kids. Since she was the choir director and later an occasional preacher, she was there, and she wanted us with her.

I didn't always welcome this constant obligation to the church community. We boys would rather be playing some basketball. Thank goodness, however, that we stayed as much as we did. Those experiences laid a foundation and instilled in me faith in Jesus Christ and the power of prayer. Mom believed deeply in those two things. She prayed in response to nearly everything. When you came to mother for advice, her first response was, "Have you prayed about it? You should work as if everything depends upon you, and pray as if everything depends on God."

When that advice didn't cover it, she turned to encouraging words: "Anything is possible if you put your mind to it!" Or "Attitude determines altitude."

Goodness knows she needed reassurance herself at times. Her job must have been enormously draining. To work as a public health nurse with the Camden Board of Social Services, she would have seen the worst of America's poverty. Her job consisted of helping others through daily existences marred by drugs, despair, and illness. She served crackheads and depressed elderly patients. Her job required a level of composure even as others were stressed or strung out. She brought this trait home; her most reassuring quality was this sense of calm. For those years when my dad was sick, Mom very well could have dipped into despair and anxiety. She did not. Not only did she hold it together, she constantly spoke of her life as a blessing. How frequently in life do those that face great hardship feel the most blessed? She spent countless hours donating her time and money to worthy causes without ever asking anything in return.

A genuine disciple, she didn't think about how much time she devoted to such causes. She just thought of things that needed to be done, and then she did them. She had goals in mind for her family and never deviated from those goals. As she soldiered on towards them, Mom never shied away from sacrifice.

In her honor, I host a dinner every year called the Tender Heart Luncheon. This event honors mothers who have children with a chronic illness. It offers those moms a chance to come together and share, to comfort and encourage. It is the kind of day that I believe my mother deserved every day. To lighten the mood a bit, I always share some of the funny things that my mother taught me, lines I read once in a poem by Bert Christenson called, "Things My Mother Taught Me,"

> *My mother taught me TO APPRECIATE A JOB
> WELL DONE.*
> *"If you're going to kill each other, do it outside. I just
> finished cleaning."*
>
> *My mother taught me RELIGION.*
> *"You better pray that will come out of the carpet."*
>
> *My mother taught me about TIME TRAVEL.*
> *"If you don't straighten up, I'm going to knock you
> into the middle of next week!"*
>
> *My mother taught me LOGIC.*
> *"Because I said so, that's why."*

My mother taught me MORE LOGIC.
'If you fall out of that swing and break your neck,
you're not going to the store with me."

My mother taught me FORESIGHT.
"Make sure you wear clean underwear, in case you're
in an accident."

My mother taught me IRONY.
"Keep crying, and I'll give you something to cry
about."

My mother taught me about the science of OSMOSIS.
"Shut your mouth and eat your supper."

My mother taught me about WEATHER.
"This room of yours looks as if a tornado went
through it."

My mother taught me about ANTICIPATION.
"Just wait until we get home."

My mother taught me ESP.
"Put your sweater on; don't you think I know when
you are cold?"

My mother taught me HUMOR.
"When that lawn mower cuts off your toes, don't
come running to me."

My mother taught me WISDOM.
"When you get to be my age, you'll understand."

This poem always gets a laugh with the women at the luncheon, even if not all of those lines point straight to my mom. After this lighthearted joking, I talk about the amazement that a son can feel for his mother's steady commitment. We aren't always mature enough to realize it or say thanks when we are young, but the best lessons I learned from Mom came simply from her resilient presence. Moms don't always do the most glamorous jobs in a family. Washing and folding clothes, shuttling kids in carpool, making the meals…these aren't often the subject of poems or movies about greatness. But the moms at Tender Heart Luncheon, like my mom, are so often the backbone of families during times of turmoil or strife. They are truly great.

Without Mom, I would not have been sitting on that plane heading down to Miami. Who knows where I would have ended up, if when Dad had to go for treatment, she hadn't managed to support all of us both emotionally and financially? How she managed to do it all, I'll never know. But she would be so proud if she were still here. I can hear her now saying in that positive tone, "Attitude determines your altitude." Well, I'm sky high, Mommy, sky high!

"Hey, yo, Gary." A knock on my arm once again snaps me out of my daydreaming.

"What is that brace on your arm, man? You gonna be able to go for the big game?"

• • • • •

"This brace, man? This is nothing. Of course I'm going to play. When you grow up playing against bigger and faster competition, in the streets no less, a little strain doesn't even cross your mind in a big game like this."

"You sure about that arm, Gary? That looked bad the night of the AFC Championship game. I can't believe you played through it. What happened anyway?"

"I hurt it on a Wham. The guard whiffed on the tackle, and Booger [Anthony McFarland] made a great play and wrapped up the running back. I had my arms around him finishing the tackle, and somebody hit me with their facemask right in the funny bone."

"Dang, but you good to go now?"

"Yeah, I'm sure, man. No way I'm missing this game."

As I reassured my teammates about my status, I thought repeatedly of a quote from the great Vince Lombardi, "No crime in getting knocked down as long as you get back up."

Well, I grew up getting knocked down. That's what comes from playing with older kids. But those knocks taught me what I could take, and that no matter what, I always had the ability to get back up. This arm injury was nothing.

Football always appealed to my rambunctious nature as a kid. I liked contact from the beginning. Playing against Grant, Greg, Granville, and their older, faster, and stronger friends gave me an advantage against my peers as I geared up for finally playing against folks my own age.

Not only was I not afraid, I was also eager to hit people and, in the words of a former coach, "Stick your face in the fan!" But my excitement about playing was soon dampened by a new reality: I was too big for the Glassboro Midget League.

In the years of my youth, midget (or pee wee) football had weight limits by age. By the eighth grade I was 140 pounds, not huge but certainly bigger than most of the kids my age; league rules stated you had to be at 130 pounds or less to play. Even after running around for weeks with trash bags on my torso in order to prompt more sweating, I still couldn't make weight. I had to wait a year for freshman football, which had no weight requirements.

During the summer, my brothers kept me in shape, and in turn I watched them play the following season. Gregory was a senior and Grant was a sophomore. Every time I watched a game, my pride grew. Greg was an absolute beast. He played both offense and defense. From the public announcer's regular crediting of his number, Greg seemed to be involved in almost every play on the field. The PA must have tired of calling the same number again and again, but as a younger brother I couldn't get enough.

While Greg was excelling on varsity that year, I spent the season on the freshman and JV teams. Between playing linebacker and running back, I had over thirty touchdowns and countless tackles. With this success, I looked forward to my sophomore year. I did the math, had my confidence, and figured that the following year I could equal that total on the JV squad alone. It might sound funny for a defensive player to be so hungry for TDs, but crossing the goal line was the best way to get girls. The casual football fan (and many high school girls fit that description) only knows the players who reach the end zone. In order to score girls in the stands, I needed to score on the field!

Though the glories of the football field always called, I also gravitated towards basketball. My dreams of playing in the NFL never diminished, but if that failed, I at least wanted to be a professional athlete of some sort. Since I was a realist, and since I was aware of my small stature, I knew that my best shot might be on the court rather than the field. Also, basketball is one of those games that you can practice by yourself. It was so soothing for my

stressed nerves to go out and shoot a few hoops in the park down the street from our house. I was the point guard all the way up to my freshman year in high school. The best thing about playing point is that you get to call your own play. My teammates always clowned me saying they knew what number I was going to call out. One finger was isolation, so I wore out that index finger. Why call the play for anyone but me? When I raised that one finger, I knew that I was going to be central to the play. Our coaches made sure things were fun by letting us use the "run and gun" offense. My favorite coaching lesson from those years, "When you are on, shoot. When you're off, shoot 'til you're on." This taught me that there was always another trip down the court, always another opportunity to excel, and so fear about success or failure was unnecessary.

My other athletic experiences saw fewer highlights. In baseball, because field space was a bit limited, we would do a period of practice in the batting cages. The coaches told us all the same thing: *let it rip.* That advice might have rung too literally in my ears, because I almost ripped my arms out of their sockets with every swing. Personally, I viewed heading back to the dugout after an at-bat without having swung the bat as just about the worst thing in the world. So, I was rarely cheated on my swings, and it perhaps affected my success rate. Some hitters bat for average. Not me. I channeled my inner Mike Schmidt, the Philadelphia Philly all-star at the time, and swung for the fences. Only one problem: I wasn't Mike Schmidt. At the plate, I missed more than I connected. In the field, though, I could cover ground and had a pretty good eye for making plays on the ball. In these ways, baseball is a great game to teach persistence. After all, even the best batters are only successful 30 percent of the time.

When hits weren't coming for me, I found entertainment in unusual things on the diamond. One thing I enjoyed was trying to steal home. Younger players usually can't throw and catch well, and success could often be found through forcing those players to execute even routine throws twice in a row. So, I'd bluff steal from third, and when the pitcher threw it to the third baseman, I'd take off for home plate. You could count on the opposition making an error somewhere along the line. These kinds of things made baseball fun, but as I got older and played on some bad teams, things grew a bit less enjoyable. Over time, even stealing home lost its magic. The football field began to loom larger and larger in my imagination. While watching my brothers play on the high school team, I started to dream of following in their footsteps. Not only that, I began to dream bigger. In the back of my mind, though I'd hardly have talked about it much, I began to dream of the NFL.

The summer after my freshman year of high school, and before my great year of thirty touchdowns, I went on a vacation with my best buddy at the time, Brian Tripp. Football practice was slated to begin the second weekend in August, and we were going on trip the last weekend of July. The Tripps were like a second family to me at the time, and Brian was like a brother. Brian and I spent most of our weekends together, played on sport teams together, and got along well. We spent many of those weekends at his house. His father was a gynecologist, so they lived differently than my family.

We loaded up in the Tripp car and headed down to Myrtle Beach, South Carolina. It was my first time away from family for an extended time; I had a blast. We ate sea food, boogie boarded on the waves, and threw the football out on the beach. We were scheduled to be on vacation for a week. But as that first week came to a close, we were having so much fun they wanted to extend their trip for another week. I was living large as a guest dependent on my hosts' plans. Who was I to protest? After telling my parents of our plan to stay, they agreed it was fine. The only problem was that football started four days before I got home. For each of those four days the coaches called my parents every day questioning my whereabouts.

When I finally got back home and went to practice, the coaches were livid. They brought me into the old office with frayed carpeting and desks from the 1960s. Before the head coach arrived, I stood glancing around this room covered in pictures of successful players, championship teams. The head coach reamed me out, calling me selfish and criticizing me with comparisons to my brother Greg. Comparisons in which I was found wanting. The pictures and trophies around that old office made me even more intimidated. These guys, from those signs of success, knew what they were talking about.

"Greg was the leader of this team. In fact, both the coaches and his teammates picked him as captain. He was always first to practice, and when he was here, he was working his butt off. Now here you come, next in line, nonchalantly strolling in for practice four days late."

Another coach chimed in, "You'll be lucky if you ever see the varsity sidelines. It'll be JV for you until you fix your attitude. These conditioning sessions are not optional, young man."

Despite the slight intimidation I felt at being the subject of their disdain, and the authority granted to them by the trophies and experience, if they were looking to hurt my feelings or motivate me, they failed. My plan all along had been to play JV, score some touchdowns, and get the girls' attention. I didn't yet know that the best way to lead was by example, and perhaps I just didn't think of myself as a leader. In retrospect, I can understand the coaches' frustration. After all, it is the attitude of the players, not their skills, that is the biggest factor in determining wins and losses.

It didn't take the coaches long to experience a change of heart about my role. With that change I got a taste of success in football that forever changed me. The Glassboro Bulldogs opened the 1996 season against our archrival Salem. This game takes place every year early in the season, and since we share a district with Salem, the winner usually takes a big step towards the playoffs with a victory. During this 1996 contest, the guy playing ahead of me at the time, a junior, made a bad read on a play. In a fit of exasperation, the coach yanked him, "Ryans, get out of there. You! Brackett, get into the game."

He gave me the play and what might have passed for encouragement, "Don't screw anything up out there, Gary."

Are you kidding me, I thought, *I'm playing varsity in the first game of the year!*

"Gary, hustle up. What's the play?"

I stared at Grant as he asked me again, "Gary? The play?" My head was spinning. *What a dream!* I looked over and saw Greg watching from the stands. I didn't worry. I knew what to do from days in the yard with my brothers. See the ball and get the ball. I figured, what the heck, I am only in for one play. The play was a power play. So I did what any novice would do on their first play of varsity, I blitzed! It wasn't a huddle call, but I was so excited to be on the field and jacked up on adrenaline. At the snap, I broke through a hole and made a tackle for a five-yard loss. I jumped up yelling and pumping my chest, sure that I had my highlight for the day. Excitedly, I started to jog back towards the sideline.

"What are you doing, Gary?" Coach yelled, "Stay on! Get back in the game!"

Aware that I didn't know the signals, or anticipating my fears, he shouted, "Just tackle the guy with the ball."

Now! I thought, *finally a coach who talks my language.*

The game ended and the stat line included fifteen tackles for G. Brackett, the younger one! Perhaps more important for the coaches, we won the game 14-6. In the process, they found themselves a new linebacker.

"Gary, you played well. We need to work on those preemptive blitzes, but I like the effort." As Coach showered down this praise, I noticed something out of my peripheral vision. The Salem coach was making a direct line to us and shouting on his way.

"I'm reporting you guys to the New Jersey Board of Athletics. You have a nineteen-year-old boy out here playing against my kids. Greg Brackett has played for four years already. He was a senior last year! Why in the world is Greg Brackett back on the field this year?"

I looked down at my jersey and immediately understood the confusion. To save money I was wearing my brother's old jersey. Brackett, #32. It had all the wear and tear that comes to a jersey worn by an active player. My coach looked at Salem's coach and said with a sly grin, "You got it all wrong. This isn't Greg. Let me introduce you to his brother Gary. He's a sophomore. You'll be seeing him for two more years." That poor Salem coach's face turned the color of a tomato, and he stormed away.

• • • • •

The accolades began to stream in after that Salem game. In response to that continual praise, and probably to temper my growing ego, my mom always reminded me kindly, "You're never as good as everyone tells you when you win, and you're never as bad as they say when you lose. Keep your perspective."

Mom was absolutely right. Winning and playing well takes talent. To do it game in and game out takes character. The thrill of playing well against good competition gave me the juice I needed to work hard. I found out what I was truly made of. Football seasons reveal character; they don't build it. The weight room and the practice field are the two places where I would build my character, physique, and talent in the years to come! After my junior year and leading into my senior year, my head coach assured me I would get a scholarship. If only he was right.

"May I have your attention please? We have begun our initial descent into Miami International Airport. Weather in Miami this evening: there's a slight wind out of the south, clear skies with no clouds and a pleasant 78 degrees."

With this news, as we had just left a snowy 18-degree Indianapolis only a couple hours before, the plane erupted with excitement. Cato and I looked at each other and smiled. After all these years, here we were. *Miami*!

He leaned over and said to me, "Money?"

I responded with our trademark response for big games, "Yea, Money."

He smiled big and laughed big. I always enjoyed Cato's laugh. It was a big belly laugh that often earned him odd looks from people at nearby tables in restaurants.

"Please return your seat backs to the upright and locked position. Flight attendants, prepare the plane for landing."

Anticipating a mob scene upon disembarking, I made sure to have my camera ready. When I came down the plane's steps, I wondered with a laugh who had forgotten the red carpet. Cameras and news crews were everywhere—the only people missing were Hollywood celebrities in designer dresses. The reporters were not allowed to talk with us on this occasion, but I guess every news station wanted to lead that night with a story about the

Colts arriving in Miami for their week of Super Bowl preparation.

We arrived later than our opponent, the Chicago Bears, as Colts' management had chosen the latest date possible to come down. We didn't want the business of this trip to get overshadowed by the scenery and distractions of South Beach. There would be time for that later, and celebrating as Super Bowl champs in Miami would be infinitely better than celebrating as AFC champs.

Walking straight from the plane to the team bus, I was intercepted by one of our PR guys, Vernon Cheeks.

"What's up, Vern?"

"What up, Captain… just reminding you that you have to do interviews once we get to the hotel."

"Yeah, I know."

My reluctance, or at least lack of excitement, was based on history. During the regular season, we have interviews after the game. Because those games are usually covered by a single news crew, one player at a time interviews at the podium and we go in order of seniority. Because I am younger, I always followed Peyton, Jeff Saturday, and Dwight Freeney. By the time we finish with questions and comments, the hour had grown late. On road trips I often couldn't go out with the rest of the guys because my interview session ran so long.

Those of us slated for interviews in Miami were pulled aside as soon as we arrived in the hotel. We followed the PR people to a ballroom toward the rear of the hotel. As we entered, loads of reporters were ready and eager to fire off questions. A series of podiums surrounded the room, the biggest one with the nameplate: "Peyton Manning — QB, Indianapolis Colts." This center podium was bordered around the room by tables with nametags. As I sat down at my table, I remembered the lessons drilled into me through both experience and PR guys like Vernon.

On your guard, Gary. Nothing for the other team's bulletin board.

Vern helped pick the questioners, and the first reporter he called on asked an easy starter, "Gary, how was the plane trip?"

"It was great. The guys were all excited to come down. Everybody was dressed in his Sunday finest. The mood was good, but the styles were even better."

"Next question," Vern prompted.

"Gary, what are you guys gonna do when you LOSE the Super Bowl?"

"Hah! You must be a Chicago reporter. I keep thinking of Dennis Green's famous meltdown, when he shouted in that press conference, *'They are who we thought they were.'* Well, the Bears are who we think they are! Seriously, though, we expect a very tough game. The Bears are running the ball well and Rex Grossman is playing really good for them."

As Vern called upon the next reporter, I recognized a face from back in my New Jersey days.

"Gary, you have gone from an all-state high school player who had to walk on in college to an undrafted free agent in the NFL, and now to this podium in Miami where you are a captain and leader of a Super Bowl team. How does that happen? Did you ever reach a point where you doubted that you would get where you wanted?"

"Well, it was a *long* tough road, but I wouldn't change a thing. I think the first real difficulty I encountered came from something that should have been positive. My junior year in high school, letters started rolling in from colleges around New Jersey. I was high as a kite and thought that with all these schools interested, I was bound to play college ball. My high school coach, Cleary, contributed to this optimism. He told me, 'Don't worry about scholarships, Gary. You just worry about playing football and I'll worry about getting you a scholarship. But with the way you're capable of playing, I'll bet my house you'll get a free ride.'"

This flattery and these compliments made me feel great. But they did not do anything more than that. What my coach failed to do was do anything on a practical level to help me pursue the dream. I didn't know that I needed to respond to those letters, and if he knew, he didn't tell me. I had some vague idea that by playing well and being so desirable to colleges, that they would come and take me by the hand, essentially ushering me to a freshman dorm. But I was not heralded enough to have colleges knocking down my door. For recruits that were somewhat on the border, colleges looked for kids to reciprocate interest. That is, I needed to let them know that I was interested, but I did not.

So heading into my senior year, I was not on the radar of many schools. Coach actually worked to get some schools to come watch a playoff game my senior year. But when I finally did get to Rutgers, I learned that most of those players were actively working on making connections with colleges by tenth or eleventh grade. Hindsight is always 20/20, but I had lost valuable time in expressing interest in schools and maximizing my chances. I ended up not getting a scholarship, though somehow Coach Cleary ended up keeping his house. Funny how that happens.

Those teams that started recruiting later, or picked up those players falling through the Division I cracks, were mostly small colleges like Towson, Wesley, and Richmond. These were all good schools, but they did not square with my dream of playing Division I football. At one point, I thought all my fears were going to be resolved with one fell swoop. Coach interrupted my daydreaming in math class when he came through the door and said, "Excuse me, Mr. Chapman, I need to see Gary for a minute."

When I got out into the hall, he said, "There are some coaches here from Syracuse, and they are interested in you."

My excitement was surely visible, and I went to talk with them.

They said, "We saw you in one of your playoff games and were really impressed. We were actually at the game recruiting a kid from Woodbury named Lamar Stardvent." Lamar was a running back/safety, a good player, and I knew he had a bunch of offers.

"We'll be honest with you. We wish we had known about you earlier. We are now out of scholarships, but if Lamar signs somewhere else, and the chances of this seem high since he has about twenty other offers, we want you to come join the Syracuse Orange."

So I rested all my hopes on Syracuse. And wouldn't you know it—Lamar chose Syracuse over all those other offers, leaving me out in the cold. The ironic thing about it, he never even showed up on campus. He was drafted as a baseball prospect and chose that route over college. His decision hardly

helped me. At that point, I was done with my senior season and had no deals on the table. Prep schools came calling, but that was not really what I wanted. Typically kids who go to those kinds of places do so because they have some academic problems. My grades were pretty good, although there was one course that didn't help my status. Spanish 2 met after lunch, and I was in danger of failing, a fact representative of me being sick of school more than anything. But because of that grade, those schools that were thinking about taking a shot on me had another reason to look elsewhere. The NCAA's eligibility requirements, known at the time as Prop 48, tended to impact a school's recruiting choices. Doubts about my eligibility were probably a final straw for Division I recruiters.

So where did all this leave me? I guessed there was always Rowan College. Rowan is a small D-III school right across the street from my high school. I took "unofficial" recruiting visits frequently during off periods. The football program was solid at the time; in fact they were fresh off a trip to the D-III finals. At the time, an assistant coach from Rowan was one of our gym teachers at the school. Aware of the problems I faced, he insisted, "Rowan would love to have you. You'll be their starting rover next year. Your speed and quickness make you a prime candidate for that spot. We think you'd be great in dropping back for pass coverage, and in coming up to make hits, too. And, who knows, we might even use you as a short yardage back so you get to play both ways."

But Rowan didn't do two things: it didn't give me a chance to play against the best competition in college at the Division I level, and perhaps just as important, it didn't get me out of Glassboro. I needed another option. Since none of my family had ever really been through this process, I had no one to ask for advice about the traditional route. I did talk to my brother Greg a good bit about coming down to visit him at his school. Greg was big on me attending a four-year university, but as my options dried up, he started to warm up to me joining him down at The Apprentice School in Newport News, Virginia. He had planned from early on to be a welder and had chosen his high school courses accordingly. If I joined my brother there, I could learn a trade like welding, mechanics, or even take courses in engineering. Even better, I could earn money while I did so. My buddy Rashaun and I decided to visit. We talked a good bit about playing football there, rooming together, and together escaping our roots in Glassboro. Even though I was unsatisfied with the quality of the football program, the idea of rooming with my old buddy was appealing. We thought that as guys with strong hands and backs, we could eventually make a good living if we went down this path. We'd known each other since the 8th grade, when we met playing pick-up basketball. Since then, we'd played sports together, flirted with girls together, and generally been inseparable. We'd have fun side-by-side in college for sure!

As I began to resign myself more and more to the possibility of either Rowan or The Apprentice School, I was called into the coach's office one day to talk to some visitors from Rutgers. I met a guy named Rod Sharpless, an older black man with a thick southern accent.

"Gary, I've got some good news and bad news for ya. Which do you want first?"

"The good news, Mr. Sharpless."

"Well, the good news is that I can get you into Rutgers. The bad news is that you are going to have to walk-on. We are out of scholarships, but we want to give you a chance to earn one over time."

I didn't know much about Rutgers. With a little research, I found out one thing for sure: they were not very good at football. For someone with a lot of choices, this might have been a negative. But, when I talked with my dad, he spun it as a positive.

"First of all, you aren't going there with a primary goal of playing football. It is a good school and that is what your priority should be anyway. But you might also think about it this way: it'll be easier to see the field for a team like that than a Miami or Notre Dame."

I considered that and agreed with at least one part. If they weren't winning much, they probably didn't have the best athletes, which gave me an even better shot! This was my rationale as I eagerly pursued this chance.

Mr. Sharpless explained a program called the EOF, or Equal Opportunity Fund, that would help me get accepted to Rutgers. Because of my family history and the fact that no one in my family had graduated college, I would be given a chance to be the first. Both of my parents considered it a great opportunity. I would be close enough so that they could still see me play, but far enough from Glassboro to avoid distractions.

I was excited at the chance to play D-I ball, get a scholarship, and attend a solid school. They might not have had the best football team, but Rutgers was known in our community as a place where you could get a great education. I was set.

As apart of the EOF program, I was required to go to classes for a month in the summer to prepare for college. At Rutgers, I joined about thirty other EOF students to take basic college courses and seminars on study skills and organizational techniques that prepared us for the academic expectations at Rutgers. Because this was a state-funded program, it was required to retain a certain number of kids each year in order to keep their funding. This fact led to something of a standoff between the EOF people and football coaches.

Dean Frazier Foster and Coach Sharpless had several conversations during that summer about whether or not I should play football my freshman year. Dean Frazer argued that I shouldn't for two reasons.

"First and foremost, Coach, Gary is a reflection of our program. If he walks on this first semester, I worry that his schedule would be too heavy. To keep up with his classes, practice and conditioning, and the EOF would be too much for any mortal to handle. Second, he has to fill out his FAFSA and do some thinking about how he will pay for school next year."

"Well, Dean, if he earns a scholarship that will solve the problem of funding."

"Coach, I'm telling you, he needs a year to get his feet set."

As I sat and listened, I couldn't help but be a bit surprised at the direction of the conversation. I thought I would be able to go and compete immediately to gain a scholarship. If I couldn't play my first year, I wouldn't be able to get a scholarship. But the only reason I was at Rutgers was because of EOF so I couldn't argue much with the dean of the program.

Even though I had doubts, I told my parents that they didn't have to worry about paying for school. I thought that after I'd been admitted, Rutgers would figure out some way for me to stay there. Boy, was I wrong. My parents filled out the FAFSA and the subsequent news was nothing short of devastating. I received absolutely zero financial aid. Because of my father's military benefits and my parents' combined income, and because my brothers were no longer dependents on my parents' income, we didn't qualify for financial assistance. But, like so many families, the fact that we didn't qualify for aid didn't mean we didn't need it like crazy. Only one option was left. Someone would have to take out loans.

They never made a big deal about it in front of me, but I know that Mom and Dad must have had some long nights talking about details and the feasibility of my attending Rutgers. The only way they were able to get the money required for school was if they refinanced their biggest asset—the mortgage on their house. They must have been skeptical about the wisdom of this risk. After all, they were 0-3 with my brothers. Each had failed out of school. Mom, as was so often the case, turned to her faith. The Bible tells how David, too, was the youngest child, and how this young boy slew Goliath. Maybe I could do the same.

In my case, the giant to be slain was the workload and responsibilities of college, and afterward I would stand victorious with a degree rather than a slingshot. We agreed that they would refinance and get me the money...but with a condition. If my grades didn't measure up, the deal was off and I was coming back home to attend Rowan. There, I would benefit from local scholarships and the football team would supplement the rest of what I needed to pay for tuition. I wouldn't have to pay for room and board because I'd just live at home. I agreed with their ultimatum. Throughout this whole process they didn't talk once about me playing football. Their main concern was that I get a good education.

After the summer of EOF prep courses, I returned to Glassboro for a couple weeks. But the time of my permanent move to New Brunswick quickly approached. My parents planned on helping me move. Rutgers check-in was at 8:00 a.m., but my father the Marine ordered that we leave the house at 4:00 a.m., even though Rutgers was only about an hour and a half from our house in Glassboro. It probably goes without saying that we were the first people in line for check-in.

When I finally did get my room assignment, Rutgers upperclassmen were there to help the freshmen move in. It was a tiny dorm room with space for two beds, a desk, and a tiny refrigerator. Since I was so early, I had first dibs on which bed I wanted. There wasn't much more in the room to choose. Luckily, my wardrobe wasn't too advanced at the time, because the closets had space enough for approximately a week's worth of clothes. Some of the students had the great idea of bunking their beds to get more room for a couch or chair. Such techniques just distracted their creators from the obvious; these rooms were about as comfortable as the age-old mattresses we had to sleep on.

By 8:30 that morning, I had moved in and was getting ready to say goodbye to my parents. Both of them agreed during the drive there that they wouldn't give me any money, given how tight things were around the house. Neither upheld the agreement.

My mom was first to tell me bye. After she helped me make up the bed and get things set in the room, she hugged me, told me that she loved me, and slipped $150 into my hand. I went outside to say bye to my father. Due to his heart condition and schizophrenia, he had decided that outside would be safer than inside with a bunch of emotional pimple-faced kids. As Mom got into the car, Dad called me to the side. He said to my mother, "We'll be back in just a bit."

We walked the sidewalks near my dorm, heading over toward the academic buildings of the Cook Douglas portion of campus. Fall had arrived early that year, so we strolled under the rust orange of the massive white oaks and brilliant yellow of ginkgo trees. Dad, too, slipped me some cash, "Look, this is my last bit of cash. You know that we are taking a chance on you here. So don't screw it up."

I immediately put my head down. I was hoping for a vote of confidence, but it didn't seem like it was coming.

"Don't put your head down. Look me in the eye. I know that I can be hard on you sometimes. But I am only hard on you because I want so badly for you to succeed. I'm proud of you. I believe in you." Tears welled up in his eyes. "Now go prove me right. Regardless though, Gary, I love you."

It was the first time I'd heard those words from my father. I made up my mind to do everything in my power to earn all of them.

I blinked and glanced up, wondering if I'd answered the reporter's question too personally and was a bit embarrassed by my emotions. But no one in the room seemed to have noticed. And the questions from that same reporter pressed on.

"So who ended up winning the argument about EOF and football? Did you end up sitting out a year?"

"Yea. I sat out a full year. Academically, it was probably a good decision. But from a football perspective, it was tough. I just plain missed the game. That year marked the first year I'd been away from the sport since way back in the eighth grade...."

I did stay sharp even if away from organized football. I regularly played tackle football intramurals in a big field across from my dorm. That field was a far cry from Lucas Oil Stadium in Indianapolis or Dolphin Stadium in Miami. My campus that year was the old agricultural college, and we played football on IM fields with a backdrop of old dairy barns and still-used greenhouses.

The humble scene around the field matched, in symbolic ways, the humble play and players. Most of those poor guys were just out there just goofing off. Not me. Guys occasionally complained because I was so physical; some of the kids even quit. But there were enough athletes on the field to help me stay sharp. That song "Everybody's Working for the Weekend" absolutely applied to me. Every day seemed to serve one function first and foremost: it took me one day closer to Sunday. Sunday was when I got my fix, and my drug of choice was football. That the brand of football was a bit weaker detracted not from my enthusiasm. Who could have known that playing on these Sundays on the intramural field would propel me toward playing on Sundays in the NFL?

At the end of that first semester, I anticipated walking on the beginning of the second semester. Yet such would have been according to plan, and perhaps the fates considered that plan too easy. I had quite a few roadblocks ahead of me. For winter break I was home from college, telling everyone who would listen, "Next semester, baby. I'm back at it. Back on the football field."

I had reason to believe this, and had no way of knowing that I'd face another obstacle first. One day that break I decided to ride my bike to my brother Greg's house. There I was to meet up with my buddy Rashaun, who I hadn't seen since departing for Rutgers. I was eager to hang out with him some, check in, and make sure he wasn't bitter about me leaving him hanging about our plan to room together at The Apprentice School. Greg lived a couple blocks away, but by cutting through the woods I could save about ten minutes. I knew those old trails like the back of my hand, but I didn't anticipate the changes that take place during a winter of heavy snow and ice.

Out of nowhere, I hit a branch and flipped over the handlebars. The natural thing to do was to break my fall with my hands, but in the process I introduced my left hand to a big, jagged piece of broken glass. I picked myself up, tried not to faint as I surveyed my hand cut nearly in half, and stumbled to my brother Greg's house. He immediately took me home to my father who took me to the emergency room. As an NFL player, I have grown used to discomfort, but as an eighteen-year-old kid, the pain was unbearable. The cut reminded me of that expression "beat him all the way down to the white meat." I could see glimpses of white meat underneath the steady flow of blood. The ER docs did their best to keep me calm as they prepped the room for stitches. "You'll be OK," I was told. "This won't hurt a bit."

My father looked at them with dubious eyes and mumbled, "It sure as hell is gonna hurt, Gary. But it is supposed to hurt. When they're done with you it'll be better."

I felt so stupid and frustrated. A week after those ER docs stitched me up I still had severe pain in my hand. I went to a hand specialist who said, "It's very likely that you tore some really important ligaments and muscles in your hand. I want to do another surgery to explore and see what type of damage you've got here."

That was my first personal experience with the hospital, and it was nothing less than nerve-wracking. They made me put on a gown and removed everything the good Lord didn't bless me with. They rolled me into a cold surgery room. Why did it have to be so cold? And then some nurse had the nerve to ask, "Which hand is it that is getting the surgery?"

I looked at them and responded icily, "The one with all the bandages."

I knew they were just doing their job, but I was nervous about going under. The doctors could probably tell that I was agitated. I noticed the doctor and anesthesiologist motion to each other before they told me, "We're going to put you to sleep now."

"OK, Doc. How long will it take for me to go down?"

"Well, just start counting backward from one hundred and you can tell us how long it took afterward."

I guess their trick worked, because my last memory before waking up in the surgical wing was reaching ninety-seven. The recovery at home kept me out of school for the first week of the second semester. Since I wasn't on the team yet, I couldn't get treatment from the team trainers. Instead, I was sent off campus to a rehab center. The specialist looked at my hand with a very grave face. "If you don't get motion and full feeling back in the first two months, your use of this hand will likely be gone forever."

In the beginning I could not even reach my thumb to my finger. I spent a couple hours every night crumbling up pieces of paper and shooting those pieces into the trashcan. Rehabbing the hand, despite the intense pain, was in fact the easy part. The hard part was answering my phone and telling Coach Sharpless why I hadn't reported to training. I dodged my phone for fear of having to tell Coach the truth.

I finally visited the Hale Center and entered Coach's office to tell him what had happened. Well, I actually didn't tell him about the bike. Trying to impress him, I made up some story about how I was riding this 1100 motorcycle and some car ran me off the road. I don't know why I thought this was more likely to earn it, but I hoped he would have some sympathy for me. He did not. "You know how dumb that sounds to me, Brackett? You better not make me look bad. I fought for you to be here. So your choices reflect on me now. As soon as you are healthy, get your ass over here to start working out."

It took about three months to regain full motion and be cleared to lift weights. Every day felt longer than the one before, and during those months I didn't even have the intramural games as an outlet anymore. Despite my anxiety, slowly but surely, my fingers got closer to that thumb, and I started making more and more shots in the trashcan.

When I finally did make my way back to the weight room to start working out, my first day back did not go as expected. Upon arriving to work out with the team, a coach broke the news that because of my schedule I had to work out when the team was finished. This college weight room was a totally new universe for me. Compared to our old high school room, the space itself was huge and the equipment looked top-notch. But it wasn't just the space that was different. I saw the tail end of the last group's work out that day and was amazed. The strength coach, a 315-pound, six-foot tall, bald, loudmouth named Skip Fuller, was yelling things I hadn't heard before.

I was given a card with some exercises and told to get after it. First on that list was something called "Hang Clean," a lift I'd never tried back at Glassboro High School. I was able to watch the more experienced players. When they were done, I stepped up on a platform to give it a go. Unfortunately, this particular lift was not nearly as easy as the last group had made it look. As I was in the middle of this poor imitation of a hang clean, Coach Fuller emerged from his office.

Surely he sees that I'm struggling with this and will help me do it. He is the strength and conditioning coach after all.

"Hey you!" he shouted.

"Yes, Coach."

"Can you read?"

I didn't really understand what he was asking and stared at him.

He said again, "I asked you: can you read?"

Reluctantly and without an iota of confidence I offered, "Uh… Yeah, I can read."

"Well, I have my doubts. If you can read, you could read this platform right here that says, 'All Big East Players Only.' I don't know who the hell you are, but I know for sure you ain't All Big East."

With this, he picked up the bar I'd been struggling with, weights and all, and tossed it toward one of the other platforms for the lesser athletes. As it clanged on the ground, he turned his back on me and silently walked back to his office.

If I had ever been so embarrassed in my life, I couldn't remember. The only other kid in the room was LJ Smith, who wasn't working out with the team because he was a Prop 48. I looked in his direction and saw him chuckling. From that point on, when I worked out with LJ, I knew to steer clear of the "All Big East" platform.

Three months later, the second semester had come and gone and I wasn't any closer to getting my scholarship. The good news was that my grades were still fairly solid. When summer arrived, my parents were at least proud that I was able to keep my GPA above a 3.0.

During the summer, most scholarship athletes stayed at school and worked out with the team. They'd take an extra class or two and work jobs to earn some spending money. However, I couldn't afford to stay at Rutgers since I would have had to pay for lodging. So I went back to Glassboro to get a job with a construction company. In my high school days I had played a bit of baseball and basketball with Frank Speaz, the owner of the company's oldest son. He set me up with a summer job so I could earn some money. Since my parents paid all they had for my tuition, it was even more imperative that I earn a bit myself.

I had no spending money whatsoever. I wasn't just broke—I owed people money. When I complained of this fact to Mom and Dad, my father tried to put a positive spin on it, "As long as you owe them, they're never broke. You are doing them a favor." That summer I made enough money to buy a hot used ride—a 1990 sky blue Hyundai Excel (the little ugly hatchback model). It looked a bit less than good, and wasn't exactly the best ride for the New Jersey turnpike.

Toward the end of that summer, I received a call from Coach Sharpless, "How is your summer coming, Gary?"

"Fine, Coach."

"I want you to try to come up to school next week to participate in some conditioning tests."

"I'll be there."

I drove that blue Excel up to Rutgers, though no faster than 60 m.p.h. Anything faster led to shaking and rattling that stirred deep fears and concerns. When I arrived, I recognized immediately my status as something of a unique situation. Everybody else had been there for the summer working out together and they were in peak shape. Sixty hours of construction may have been good for the wallet, but it certainly hadn't been good for the body. Usually after a day of work I was too tired to run, so I had skipped more workouts than I had completed.

The day I arrived, they paired us up to get our 40 times. They had me run my first 40 with the kicker. He was pretty athletic, but still...a kicker. I felt a bit insulted by the coach's pairing, but decided to roll with it. Guys on the team chose sides with each pairing, and because it would be funny to watch the kicker outrun someone, they almost universally rooted for him. I finished at about 4.7 seconds and the kicker came in about 4.9. To run next to the kicker actually made me look a bit faster, and after I finished I could hear folks talking

"Who is that guy?"

"I don't know, you know him?"

One of Rutgers's most well-known players, a star running back named Dennis Thomas, spoke up: "Yeah, I know him. I played against him in high school. My team, Salem, lost to his Glassboro squad in the playoffs. The guy can play I tell you."

I chuckled to myself when I heard him talking, remembering his angry coach who accused us of cheating, *What are you thinking letting a nineteen-year-old kid play against high school kids? Greg Brackett has been playing for four years!*

I went over to Dennis, eager to say hello. Because of his status on the team, he gave me instant creditability. He told the other guys how I had a stellar high school career but somehow didn't get a scholarship. The rest of the day I tested pretty well for not working out and even outran some of the scholarship linebackers. In future weeks, I was glad that I came to the testing for one reason in particular. Getting to know Dennis and some of the other players helped me a bunch.

I hung out with those guys the days before practice began. They dreaded, and didn't stop talking about, the *110 Test*. In this test, we had to complete sixteen sprints of 110 yards in less than seventeen seconds. We had thirty seconds rest in-between with a running clock, so it ends up testing both endurance and speed. Since I had not been running like I was supposed to, I worried about this test in particular. The night before the test we had a team meeting. There, the coaches spoke about their expectations for the year. Because of high expectations, they wanted everyone to pass the *110 Test*. If we could do it, we would be the first Rutgers team to ever pull it off.

Better than that feeling of exclusivity, universal success would mean that every player was done with this terrible experience. After all, if you fail the test you have to wake up an hour earlier and run the test every day until you pass it. Coach Sharpless spoke up, "Tomorrow is y'all's *110 Test*. And you guys had better be ready. And I don't want to hear that y'all ain't ready. Only reason you ain't ready is if you dead or something."

The room chuckled, but the mood was tense. Everyone knew it wasn't going to be fun. Since it was new to me, I had no idea how to run this test. The first sprint I went as hard as I possibly could, wanting to show everybody that I was there for business. Only Coach Sharpless knew about me, so I'm guessing that first sprint surprised some folks. The guys warned me though, "You better slow down."

"That's not the right pace, man."

"You aren't going to have enough left at the end."

Ah…they just want me to take it easy on them and not make them look bad.

The second sprint I went just as hard, but at about yard fifty I grew more and more convinced that I had indeed better slow down. I ran the next eight at a decent clip, but each one grew tougher and tougher. At sprint eleven, I began to doubt that I could finish, but my refusal to admit failure kept me from quitting. The next four sprints found me crossing the line just as the timekeeper yelled, "Time." Since I was finishing on the last possible second, I had less recovery time. After I finished fifteen, I couldn't hold it in any longer. I ran to the fence behind the end zone and threw up beside the white oak trees that lined the field. The security guard standing outside the fence chuckled quietly to himself as he watched me. My lungs were on fire, and I felt like I just couldn't make it anymore. I was mid-throw up when I heard *"three, two, one, go!"* This was the last sprint, and I felt like I could probably tough it out. My biggest problem as I decided to go for it was that, since I had run off the back of the field, I had ten extra yards to go. At that exact moment, I remembered Dad's words from so long ago,

"No such thing as a try, Gary. You either do it or you fail to do it."

With that model of determination on my mind, I took off. I would not be called a quitter on my first day! The timekeeper shouted out the numbers

fourteen – I turned it up a notch

fifteen – Still 20 yards to go

sixteen – Last little bit here

seventeen – I dove as if I was scoring the winning touchdown.

I was exhausted but one of the coaches came up to me afterward. "You are in terrible shape."

"I know, Coach."

"But I like that you didn't quit. Good job."

That never-quit attitude carried me through the entire season. I always did my best. No matter how often teammates pleaded with to me to "take it easy, stop making us look bad." I wasn't going for those kinds of requests.

In my role on the scout team, I soon figured out the offense on the other side of the ball. With this knowledge I started to bust up plays in practice. So, eventually the coaches put me on the other field where the defense practiced, saying, "We want you to learn the defensive schemes. Maybe you can play some D." I felt as if the coaches were mocking me behind my back for working so hard, which did little but piss me off. *Why would they not want to see me push harder?*

Well, I already knew the defensive system, but I took this frustration as just another of the disadvantages of being a walk-on. I didn't have access to the meal rooms because I could eat more cheaply on my own than on the meal plan. I did not have access to the academic advisors.

On the field, during practice, coaches treated me differently. I got fewer chances and less leeway for mistakes. If we all had shared reps, scholarship guys received four to our two, and if I made a mistake on one of those first ones I had no second opportunity.

These disadvantages catalyzed what I later came to understand as the walk-on mentality. I began to relish obstacles and took pride in knowing how to solve problems. The lack of academic advisors gave me more freedom to pick the classes I wanted. The lack of reps meant that I had fewer reps in which to exert all my effort. So when the coaches told me "learn the schemes," I embraced my walk-on mentality and tried to do more with less.

Later in life, I came to understand the formative power of these disadvantages and obstacles. Many scholarship players are from day one never forced to do anything for themselves. They are walked through their college careers. When adversity comes, instead of facing it and overcoming it, they do what they have been taught: ask other people for help.

The lack of enthusiasm displayed toward me from the coaches didn't stop me from excelling on special teams. On our first day of practice, I saw an opportunity and seized it. When the kickoff return team was going through their reps, I volunteered to run down and give them a look. I thought that if I showed them that I could run like a raging bull, they would put me on the team. I gave the best look I could, and in so doing, I stuck out like a sore thumb. It was evident I was giving more effort than everyone else. After an injury to one of the first-team players, I received a spot on the kick-off team, which I parlayed into punt team and then all the return teams.

I took great pride in the special teams role, even though that season the team struggled to a 1–10 record. I wanted to do more, though. I wanted to play defense, and I still needed some funding.

That off-season was the first year that I worked out with the team. I felt more comfortable in lots of ways, and that comfort translated into results. I knew the coaches, knew what to expect on things like the *110 Test*, and felt like nothing could hold me back. I grew stronger and faster and maintained the same intensity in the weight room during the off-season. The strength coach and I reconciled after he grew to appreciate my attitude during the workouts.

The hard work paid off with tangible rewards. That year in the spring game, I received the award for the *Best Off-Season Workout*. Eventually I went on to set records for my position that still stand at Rutgers today. When I go into the new weight facilities at Rutgers these days, my name is up on the board as the record holder in the hang clean, shuttle run, and some others. As a walk-on, it meant a lot to be honored, and sit still means a lot today. I felt like some overdue respect was finally coming my way. Going into that next season, I was slated as a back-up linebacker and remained one of our best special team players. Things were looking up.

My growing optimism shattered upon a call from my father as camp ended. With this voice from home, my whole demeanor changed: "Gary, we did all we could. We refinanced the house twice for your college tuition, and there's no way we can come up with the money for this year's tuition payment."

I was heartbroken. Just when things were going well, I felt like someone stabbed me in the heart. But the worst part was the guilt I felt about what I knew my parents were going through. I knew that they felt even worse than I did and that they had done everything they could to come up with the money. To put your parents through that kind of heartache, to see them struggle to help, that was the hardest part. I prepared to go speak with the Rutgers coaches.

I made an appointment to speak with Coach Stekel, my position coach, to inform him that I would be leaving. We had spoken previously about a scholarship, but it didn't seem like a real option.

"Come in, Mumbles!" said Coach Steckel, "How are you?"

Coach called me Mumbles, because whenever we discussed the defense, I would mumble my answer to ensure that he wouldn't hear me if I was wrong.

"I'm not great," I said. "It has been my pleasure to play for you, but I have to inform you that I'm ... I'm leaving Monday. I cannot afford my tuition anymore."

"Don't you have any type of financial aid?"

"No sir, I don't."

"Well, it's not my decision whether you get a scholarship or not."

"Yeah, I know, I know. Nobody's fault here, just wanted to say my farewells. Actually thinking of taking off today so I can get some things in order at Rowan."

"Rowan?"

"It's in my hometown, right across from my old high school, and I know the coaches over there."

Coach knew I was serious once I mentioned an alternative. "Wait till Monday, Gary. I'll go and talk to Coach Shea and see what I can do. No promises, though."

"OK, Coach, I'll see if I can hold on till then." I knew that if the head coach at the time, Coach Shea, could be convinced, many of these financial worries would go away overnight.

That Monday morning, with a heavy heart, I started packing all of my stuff. I drove over to Scarlet Knight Way. I planned on speaking to the coach after our 8:00 a.m. workout. I was doing some squats when one of the scouts came down to the weight room and told me that the coach wanted to see me.

Lord, please let me get a scholarship.

Coach Shea was a fish out of water, a Californian coaching on the East Coast who was having a difficult time convincing his highly recruited Cal kids to follow him across the country. He meant well, but there is a difference in the aura of a Jersey guy and a man from California.

He said, "Coach Steckel tells me that you have some tough decisions to make."

"Yes, sir. Well, actually, no, sir. The decisions are already made. My parents can no longer afford tuition."

"I see. Well, Gary, you've come a long way. You were named the most improved player for the spring, which was a sign that you have a great work ethic. But Rutgers, under my coaching, will recruit players bigger and better than Gary Brackett."

At this moment, I had a tear in the corner of my eye and was struggling to stay solid. Since I thought the conversation was over, I stood up to leave.

"I'm not done. Gary, I like you! You're always early to meetings. You're doing well in school. And you do well for our scout teams. Not only that, but we just had a couple of scholarships open up. We want to offer you one."

"Are you kidding me? Thanks, Coach! I won't let you down. I promise."

My heart was racing as I left that office. Slowly it slowed down, but my excitement and enthusiasm lingered. I actually pinched myself to make sure I wasn't dreaming. Was this really happening after all those mornings of sweat and tears? Was the answer to my hopes and prayers really presenting itself right here in the Hale Center? I left Coach Shea's office ecstatic and anxious to call home. Dad and I were talking regularly at this point, and for the last couple weeks we hadn't had anything positive to talk about. I had to call my father to tell him the good news. I dialed him up from just outside the weight room.

"I've got good news, Dad."

He responded sarcastically, "You find fifteen thousand dollars to pay for your tuition?"

"Uh, well, kind of."

"What you talking about, boy?"

"He gave me a scholarship."

"Don't play wit' me."

"I'm not playing with you. I just left his office. One of the players failed out of school, and there was a scholarship open, so he gave it to me."

I could hear in my dad's voice that he was getting choked up. "You done good, boy. You done *good*."

Still excited after I got off the phone with him, I went into the weight room. Guys were in the middle of a regimented workout, moving from station to station like clockwork. I went to find the person I knew who would be most excited for me, Dennis Thomas.

"DT, I'm staying. I got a scholarship."

"South Jerz, you here!" He would always boast that South Jersey ball was better than North Jersey so now I'd be here for good to back this argument.

"What is going on here? Gary, why are you disrupting my weight room?"

"Skip! I got a scholarship!"

"Good for you. Now get back to your station and earn it. Finish your work."

As I made my way back to my station, I passed Wesley Robertson.

"Was good, Brack?"

"Man, Jerz, I got a scholarship!"

"Scholarship? Ha! Gary, you should be worried about starting…not getting any scholarship."

And so I had a new mountain to climb, but one that I faced eagerly. As a walk-on, I had never considered starting an option. Therein lies the problem we all face. We can only rise to the level of our expectations and situations. I had programmed my mind to do just enough to make the squad. I should have been programming myself, not only to make the squad, but to be a starter as well. He was exactly right. All I wanted was a scholarship and that's exactly what I got. That day I switched gears, dead set on starting.

The reporter took notes eagerly. I looked around the room at my Colts teammates, wondering how their interviews were going. Cato was to my left, navigating reporters with his typical ease. Reporters at this event dug harder than usual for stories, but I guessed things are different at the Super Bowl.

"So you got your scholarship? And weren't you named MVP your last two years at Rutgers? That is quite a progression. I guess changing your focus worked for you, huh?"

I thought about the question. It sounded so rosy, like things had gone so smoothly after that. If only such was the case. By no means were things all set from that moment in Coach Shea's office. The scholarship was a big step, but even after that I couldn't shake the coaches' perception of me as a walk-on. Under Coach Shea's staff, I was just the hard-working kid who had been too mediocre to recruit. Midway though my second year, I was playing special teams at a pretty high-level, and that line-up was easier to work into. The defensive side of the ball was tougher to crack.

Coaches always promoted the guys they recruited. This makes sense from their perspective. If a coach promised parents, coaches, and a player that he is going to get a chance to play, that coach is bound by his word to play him over some other people. That I was better, and knew I was better, was a small part of the equation. Compounding the complexity, the kid in front of me was not the only horse in the stable. If that kid came from a high school program that happened to be talent-rich, and so had future players the Rutgers coaches were eager to draw, who was more likely to play? The guy who helps sell your team to prospective talent, or the guy from Glassboro?

Despite the difficulties I faced with cracking the defensive rotation, I did play in a few games and had some highlights. At this time, the Big East was still intact, and I played against the three future ACC teams: Virginia Tech, Miami, and Boston College. The season did not end as it began. After winning only one game and losing ten the year before, Rutgers enjoyed a 2–0 start in 2000. After our early success, our confidence grew. The big test in week three was heading to Blacksburg, Virginia, and playing the Hokies of Virginia Tech, a top-five team in the country at the time. How great would it be for Rutgers to go in and shock their home crowd and the world?

Before the game the seniors pumped up the locker room as we listened to loud music. The scene reminded me of that line from *Braveheart*, "we didn't get dressed up for nothin." If we were going to reach our goal of a bowl game, we were going to have to start winning some of these big games. As we prepared, we just knew this was our year, and the Hokies were our shot. As the music and our energy reached a crescendo, Coach Shea busted in the door eager to give a memorable speech. He yelled and we responded in kind.

"Are you guys ready?"

"Yeah!"

"OK, guys, this is a big game, and because of the national TV, they asked us to go out on the field early. And I told 'em hell no! We do what we do! We don't do what others tell us to do!"

"Yeah!"

Someone in the back yelled, "This is the day we finally get some respect."

Coach Shea was, in retrospect, whistling past the graveyard. He was screaming and yelling to convince us that he was ready and wasn't scared. In fact, he was scared to death. And just like a kid tries to convince himself as he walks past the graveyard that things are fine by whistling, Coach screamed to make it seem as if he wasn't scared of what was about to happen. He screamed again, "Tell me for real! Are all you guys ready?"

"Yeah!"

"Is this a must-win game?"

"Yeah!"

At our answer, he looked at us astounded that we had responded as loudly as we had and said exactly the wrong thing. "Noooo!" he said. "This isn't a must-win game. We only have to win six games to get to a bowl."

If life and death are in the tongue, he had given us a verbal atomic bomb. With those words, the bubble burst in our locker room, and a riled-up and energetic group transformed instantly into a confused and disoriented one. Coach's message could be interpreted only one way: he didn't think we had a chance. Maybe we didn't. We lost that game 49–0. We had no shot when we headed to the field for the first half. But more important than that loss and the embarrassing score, Coach Shea lost his team.

The game in Blacksburg wasn't all bad news for me. I had what perhaps was the highlight of my college career: two sacks of Michael Vick. At the time, Vick was the most electric player in college and a Heisman candidate for best player in the country. My family would later give me grief, saying, "He didn't see you coming. If he had, you wouldn't have got him."

But in my mind, a sack was a sack. And two sacks were even better! That year we went on to win only one more game. As the year progressed, and the team regressed, Rutgers' administration began to lose patience with Coach Shea. The last straw came in an embarrassing game against Notre Dame. NBC, which covers every Notre Dame football game, actually declined to cover our game so they broadcast a more even match-up, one that would earn better ratings.

In college sports, losing is one thing. Losing money is an entirely different beast, and a much more nasty one. The writing was on the wall, and the night of that game the athletic director and coach met to discuss a letter of termination.

The next day, Coach Shea called an emergency team meeting. As we trickled into the Hale Center, we knew something big was going down. The meeting was slated for 7:00 p.m., but Coach was about 30 minutes late. He explained that he had been forced to give his resignation and wanted everyone to know that he hadn't given up on his team. In short, he stressed that he was being forced out. Coach was a likeable guy, a straight shooter who meant well, and after the meeting some of his players cried and worried that their coach had been fired. They were worried that all the things the coach had promised them on their recruiting visits might vanish with the next coaching staff.

I didn't dislike Coach Shea and felt somewhat guilty about his firing. But another part of me, if only subconsciously, knew that this was my opportunity. I would no longer be looked at like a walk-on. I would now be seen in the same light as the other players, and may even be a step closer to that goal...starting!

That year, the athletic banquet tickets cost about $100 dollars each. Because I didn't think I was getting an award, I told my parents that they didn't have to come. When I wound up winning "The Twelfth Man of the Year" and "Special Teams Player of the Year" awards, I was shocked. I called home to tell my parents. Their excitement for my achievements was tempered only by the fact that they hadn't been there to celebrate with me.

Dad said, "We want to be there for you. You have to tell us when these big events are coming up."

They vowed that they would never miss such an opportunity again. In years to come, when I won awards, Mom and Dad were right there alongside me.

The search following Coach Shea's dismissal didn't last long. Coach Greg Schiano was named new coach on December 1, 2000. Before winter break, he called his first team meeting to get a glimpse of us and to introduce himself. Coach Schiano made sense at Rutgers for multiple reasons. He arrived from the University of Miami, where he had been the defensive coordinator. When he left, Miami ranked as the top team in the country, so he knew how to coach talented players. But perhaps just as important as his professional success was his geographic background. He was from New Jersey and had a lot of ties in the state.

His goal, he told us, would be to build a wall around New Jersey, recruiting all the top players in the state, but also to use his Florida connections to get some of those players to move north. I still remember our first one-on-one meeting. I walked into to his office, "Hey, Coach. I'm Gary. Nice to meet you."

He stopped me and my enthusiasm in my tracks, "You can sit down. Now, what can I do for you?"

"I just wanted to introduce myself. Also, I wanted to mention that I was just awarded a scholarship."

"Well, I'll have to see about that."

I was frustrated, but understood what he was doing. He was trying to get his hands on as many scholarships as possible. He wanted to recruit his type of players, and he needed scholarships to do so. Also, and he said this openly, we had in his estimation about ten legitimate Division I players on our team. So his goal was to make it as hard as he could for the guys. And if they wanted to leave and give up their scholarship, he would gladly oblige.

Coach Schiano wasn't all bad news. He also told me that those guys who stuck with it, and proved themselves, would all have equal opportunity in his eyes. We didn't have any All Big East players, so no one's place on the depth chart was secure.

I tuned out the negatives and amped up the positives. They were all I needed to hear. He did mention one thing that would shape the coming months for me: "I don't know if you'll make it. But I do know that you need to lose some weight."

At the time I was about 238 pounds. Coach Shea and his staff hadn't made much of a big deal about body weight. We didn't even have to take body fat numbers. All he cared about was how much we could lift. That changed really quickly with Coach Schiano. That winter break I stayed up at college to take an extra class and to start working on slimming down. If coach wanted me slimmer, I'd get slimmer! I worked out every day with LJ. We had a good workout regimen, running and stairs in the morning, with some weights every afternoon. Marine boot camp had nothing on this! Winter break only lasted about a month, but in that time I lost about twenty pounds, ending up at 218. At the time, I was taking a weight and muscle supplement called Hydroxycut and the results were undeniable. I would finally have the chance to prove that I belonged at the D-1 level, and couldn't wait for break to be over so I could prove it: an even playing field at last.

10

When we reported back to the Hale Center after winter break, Coach Schiano assembled his entire staff for an introductory meeting. He'd made some new hires and was ready to introduce us to the new coaches. Each coach came to the podium to say a few words. They seemed to have met beforehand to agree on the mood they wanted to convey. It was one of fun intimidation; they were there to whip us into shape. There was a new sheriff in town, and it seemed that this program had become a military base over the holidays.

The two coaches with whom I would spend most of my time were the linebackers' coach and the strength and conditioning coach. Jay Butler was about six-foot-seven, in shape, and very smart. As the strength and conditioning guy, he had the activities of the weight room down to a science. The first action he took was to collect body weights and composition numbers. His findings were apparently not great, a fact to which he devoted considerable attention in team meetings,

"You guys are F.A.T....*FAT*! How are you going to compete in the Big East when you're carrying thirty extra pounds? How you gonna run down the other guys when they have more muscle and are quicker? Well, I've got some good news, gentleman. This is a problem I can solve. From here on out, we will have fat camp every morning. Those of you who are overweight get to show up earlier than the rest of the team."

Coach Butler recorded everything in the weight room, "How much you lifted? Mark it down. What did you eat today? Record it in the charts! Are you improving every week? No? Then you better step up the effort!"

Not everyone was excited about the changes. After all, we went from Easy Street to more exacting and demanding standards. I for one was excited.

Coach D'Onofrio, the linebackers' coach, brought changes with him as well. He commanded our attention because of his resume. He had been a standout linebacker at Penn State, perhaps the most prestigious school in the country when it comes to developing linebackers. After his career as a Nittany Lion, he had been selected thirty-fourth in the NFL draft, a fact he shared with us frequently. Coach D'Onofrio was an absolute perfectionist. Even if you made a good play, he rode you because it wasn't great. He was high energy and very demanding, but I was eager to please. I felt like I was always coachable. Finally, I had someone who, if I could get him to take interest in me, could really teach me and show me how to play the position.

After introductions, we players had a couple rough weeks during winter conditioning. Under Coach Shea, our routines had been fairly laid-back during this period. After all, we were still nine months from the next season. This was just a time for us to stay in shape and work a bit on our strength. But the first winter of Coach Schiano's reign was a whole new world. Every morning, we were up by 5:00 a.m., since we were expected to be on the field by 6:00 a.m. At that time, the first whistle sounded. If you weren't there, you'd have hell to pay.

Getting up early wasn't the only thing. The intensity level was extremely high. We ran sprints until we didn't think we could stand. Then we ran some more. A number of guys took this challenge as their cue to check out, walking out of the practice bubble mumbling, "This isn't what we were promised by Coach Shea."

"Yeah, this isn't what I signed up for. It ain't worth it, man."

But Rutgers was Coach Schiano's team now. He consistently reminded us, "This is a whole new program. If you aren't willing to get with it, I'm more than happy to sign those transfer papers!"

When I called home to complain about the changes, Dad reminded me to suck it up and deal. He actually brought up his own past, at least in a sideways manner,

"No one invites challenges, but we all have to face them," he told me. "You don't think that I haven't experienced developments I felt bitter about? You think you're the only person who's ever had something come up? How are you going to deal, son? Think about the positives here."

Though some players responded negatively to the new expectations, Dad's chat and the new routine actually helped me get off to a fresh start. Losing those twenty pounds over winter break made me a lot faster and stronger. After all, I wasn't carrying around an extra bowling ball of fat. I led groups in exercises and was determined to earn a starting position.

Coach had a sheet of players every day that he would designate the hardest workers for that day. Those who won that award wore a red jersey. All those who had earned a red jersey went first in drills. Completion of some of these drills was contingent on success. In other words, if one person messed up in the drill, the whole group had to do it again. Those in the red jersey group were generally more focused and harder workers. With the reds, you were less likely to have to repeat or go back in the drill.

In contrast to those harder workers, Coach Schiano had inherited a couple of players who he seemed determined to break. No matter where they fell in the line for drills, it was almost certain that they were going to have to do the drill again. This sent their entire group back to the beginning.

The drills varied. But often we'd do high knees over big bags, lateral shuffles through bags, circle drills that required you to run in tight rapid loops. Each of these required perfection from each of the twenty other guys in your group. If someone's focus lapsed... Again! The worst drill, and the one that fostered the most competitive energy, was known as the mat drill. There were typically five lines of people that had to roll, shuffle, sprint in place, spring up as high as we could, all on command and all instantly. It worked all the muscle groups but also offered a tough cardio test.

Toward the end of winter conditioning, we started going to the fields to run plays. Whoever had worked hardest during the winter conditioning would be the starters for these plays. Well, this was the first time I saw my name penciled in as the starter. All of the hard work was paying off. I just had to stick with the program.

This was easier said than done, however. First of all, the coaches were extremely demanding, and every player had good days and bad. Also, I still doubted that I could keep things up. I had been the starter for just one game under the old regime when those in front of me on the depth chart were injured. After just two mistakes in that game, I was right back on the bench. This experience shaded my perception of myself. Did I even have what it takes?

As a walk-on who had struggled, it was easy to think that I might be on a shorter leash than others. I spent a terrible amount of time worrying about messing up. This mindset plagued me on the field and off. When I was on the field, I constantly talked to myself, *Don't mess up, Gary. Just don't mess up. Please don't miss a tackle.*

But where the mind goes, the body follows. Since I spent most of my time thinking about messing up, that's exactly what tended to happen. I missed assignments. I missed tackles. I feared demotion on the depth chart. As an answer to these fears, one day Coach Schiano called me to his office after practice. I expected the "This is not working out" talk and bad news about my demotion to second string. The tenor of the conversation surprised me.

"I called you in here to tell you how much I appreciate your daily effort," he said. "You are becoming a leader on this team. (*Wow*, I thought, *me, a leader?*) You remind me a lot of Nate Webster. He played for me at Miami and is now in the pros with the Tampa Bay Buccaneers."

"Yeah, I know who Nate Webster is, Coach! Thanks for the compliment!"

"I just want to ask you something though."

"Anything."

"At times, it seems to me that you are hesitant on the field. What are you thinking about out there?"

"Well, to tell you the truth, mostly I'm just worrying about messing up.

See, I've worked so hard to get this starting role and I don't want to blow it. Also, since I wasn't a stud recruit, I feel like I am on a shorter leash. I don't feel like there is much room for error."

He looked at me, nodded, and said something that has stayed with me for the rest of my life: "Whether you think you can or think you can't, either way you're right. The power of the mind is unbelievable. Whatever you spend most of your time thinking about, that's what you are going to spend most of your time portraying."

Coach's talk convinced me that I needed to switch the way I was thinking about things. Instead of worrying about possible mistakes and missed tackles, I needed to visualize success. After that talk, I began to force myself toward positive thoughts. *Practice is going to be good today. Practice is going to go well, and every time I get the chance to make a play...I'm gonna make it!*

Coach transformed the way we thought of ourselves and the way we worked. He convinced us before that first season that Rutgers was an elite college program. He absolutely revolutionized our mindsets. Unfortunately, he couldn't do much about the lack of talent. Before Rutgers football got any better, from a record standpoint, it would get even a little worse.

We did improve in other areas though. Even if we weren't much better on the field, Coach concentrated heavily on academic success. Every morning we had a breakfast session during which we reviewed our daily schedule— classes and study plans especially—with our coaches. We had ample study hall time and academic advisors. This was really helpful, especially for those guys who were academically on the verge of failing. Some players that normally would have failed out of school received a real education because of Coach Schiano's focus on grades. Our success academically was a source of pride for the entire program, as Rutgers continually ranks high in graduation rates compared to other public universities.

This success did not extend to the field. We just flat out didn't have the talent. We were more competitive but could never get over that hump. In fact, we suffered one of the worst losses in Rutgers' history that year when we played West Virginia. We were down about 28 in the first half, a fact that was particularly embarrassing given the national TV audience watching from home. We were being beaten badly enough and early enough in the game to start dreading a very long day. On one particular play, after West Virginia scored, Coach D'Onofrio called me over to him and lit into me, "Brackett! You just let that guy block you out of the play. How does it feel to give up a touchdown? How does it feel to give up on your team and yourself?"

"We're down 35. It's not like I'm the only one who's given up."

"I'm not concerned about others, Gary. I'm talking to you. Somewhere somebody just turned on his or her TV set. And for some reason your number 41 appealed to them. So they spent the next few minutes watching you on TV. It's up to you to decide what kind of impression you want to give them. First impressions are often last impressions. That person who turned on the TV could be an NFL scout. It could be your future wife. Either way, would you want them to think of you as a quitter?"

"No, Coach," I said ruefully.

"I didn't think you would. Don't look at the scoreboard. For all purposes, it doesn't matter anyway. Play every play like the score is 0–0. Play like every play is your first and maybe your last chance to show others what kind of player you are, what kind of heart you have inside you."

We ended up losing 80–7, but that game changed the way I viewed competition. For the game, I ended up with eighteen tackles. But my personal evolution was deeper than that number. I came to understand that competing isn't just about the score. Competing means giving your best at all times, because your reputation is at stake. Reputations are what make leaders. You can't demand the best from your teammates if you aren't leading by example.

I played hard for the rest of the season and was named captain as a reward for my tireless efforts. I tried to will us toward becoming a good football team. In order to do this, I couldn't afford to have a bad practice, weight room session or performance in the classroom. My peers and coaches responded to my efforts by naming me MVP, and my parents were there to see it this time! Although the team still had a bad record at 2–9, the feeling around the Hale Center was that momentum was turning.

11

"**O**ne last question, Gary. Any mistakes you've made, any regrets that you may have about your journey?"

Chuckling, I said, "I've been talking for a while and don't think we got that type of time."

I must have had great timing, because at that moment Vern walked up behind me and said, "OK, guys. Interview is over. All of the players will be back at the podium tomorrow."

Vern's timing was lucky for me on two levels. I was exhausted, but also, I did not really want to talk about my mistakes or regrets. I had no regrets about going to college and walking on. Those experiences developed the work ethic that got me where I was. But at the same time I did a few things I wish I hadn't.

Losing so many games in college began to take its toll. When I turned twenty-one, parties became a bigger part of my after-game ritual and the coping process for all that losing. We would go out to different houses in New Brunswick. It might not have been a drinking "problem," but I drank as much as the next guy on the team. In college, that meant some binge drinking and various drinking games like beer pong. But mostly, we just drank on Saturday nights. When final exams approached the end of my junior year, my stress level increased. I had been struggling in calculus. In order to graduate and move on, I had to pass that class.

I was worried, as well, about things at home in Glassboro. I talked occasionally with my brothers, and knew that they were involved in some bad stuff. In fact, I'd been a firsthand witness during one episode. I was spending some time with my brother Greg. We had gone to the projects across from our home in Glassboro to get our hair done, preparing for a party that weekend. As we chatted in this house, someone burst in with a pistol and shot in my direction wildly. Luckily, no one was hurt, but things escalated from there.

I was not home for the next episode but heard about it in detail from my brothers. Greg had been involved in some disputes over drugs with a group of brothers, known in that area as the Williams boys. Though not directly involved, obviously the Brackett brothers all had Greg's back. We were the type of family that, right or wrong, stuck up for each other. Granville was less involved than Greg, but he proved his allegiances by starting a fight with one of the Williams boys who happened to walk in front of our house. Granville approached the Williams boy, who didn't back down, and a fistfight broke out. One of the Williams boys ran to retrieve some weapons. Greg, as he came around the corner of the house to see Granville fighting and to hear someone shouting, "get the guns," responded in kind.

When Greg emerged from the back of our house, having hurried to his stash spot for weapons, he was wearing a bulletproof vest and wielding two handguns like some kind of old-time cowboy. He arrived at the same time the Williams brothers did with their guns, and shots rang out. One of the Williames, the one fighting Granville, was hit in the leg by a shot. Everyone else dashed for cover.

When the police arrived, Greg claimed to have been defending his brother. But with a wounded guy on the ground, and an entire neighborhood of witnesses to a full-fledged gunfight, he was clearly going to spend some time in jail.

All of this took a terrible toll on my mother. She had seen Camden chew up so many people and spit them back out as fractions of a whole, and now she watched as it happened to her son. Mom had always maintained a bit of willful ignorance about Greg's involvement in the drug scene. She didn't ask about the gunshots because she knew that the guns would lead to the drugs, and that the drugs would probably lead her son to jail. When she found a bag of cocaine in his dresser drawer, she didn't argue too forcefully with his defense that it was "baby powder." She even avoided reality with her language, speaking vaguely of all evil as "that dope." She didn't differentiate between types of drugs or even bad influences. She encouraged us to avoid drugs with, "Don't you get into that dope." She warned us of alcohol, "Don't you drink that dope and get all drunk." Even girls of questionable integrity often prompted, "Don't you be hanging around and fooling around with that dope. She ain't no good."

Greg's arrest was a sort of final straw for my mother. She was depressed for weeks. For me, it was just another straw on an already overburdened camel's back. I was bound to break at some point. I vowed to focus on what I could control. After all, though I was only a couple hours away via car, I felt like I was worlds apart from my brothers and family. Nonetheless, my concerns about school did not subside, and my concerns about things back home took on an entirely new dimension late one night that May.

"Gary, sit up. I have some bad news."

"What is it, Dad?"

"Rashaun Nelson was killed yesterday. He was murdered."

I struggled to process this information.

"What?"

"From what I understand he was in Paulsboro. He was walking home, people stole his money and killed him. The paper out of Gloucester led with the story and said that it was drug related."

Memories of Rashaun and concerns for his family swam through my mind. How heartbroken must his mom be? Rashaun had always been a good friend to me. If I wasn't here at Rutgers, it is likely that we would have been together in Newport News right now. He'd been one of my best friends, and I felt guilty for having not spoken to him in a few months. I felt guilty for having chosen the path I did. For him to be gone at so young an age...words couldn't express how I felt.

Unfortunately, such tragedies from our old neighborhood were not entirely unexpected. Growing up, I knew what the drug game was about. I had dabbled in that drug scene for a little while until I realized that it would take me nowhere fast. Too many of my peers didn't make it to college, and the streets took them. As I stood in the church as a pallbearer, I considered how easily this could have been me.

I guess the death of my best friend, losing game after game at Rutgers, Greg's drug issues, and concerns about classes all added up. The next night, at a party with a bunch of fellow players, I drank far too much to drive. At the time I knew the risks of drinking and driving, but those risks weren't for me. I was above them. When I left the last party of the night, I took a shot with a friend as I made my way to the door. Somebody had taken my keys, but I rummaged through drawers until I found them and then snuck off to head home.

The next thing I remember, I was pulled over on the side of the road…

"You are under arrest for driving under the influence.

"You have the right to remain silent, anything you say can and will be used against you in a court of law…"

I zoned out as the policeman read me my Miranda rights and fell into a sea of questions. *What? How can I get back to reality? What the hell did I just get myself into? Just as things were starting to go right, and this mistake jeopardizes everything. Wait, wait, forget me! How about if I would have been in an accident and injured someone else for doing something that was so irresponsible? Dad struggled with drinking too much to cope with stress. Now am I doing the same thing?*

When my father arrived at the police station, I could tell by the look on his face that he was disappointed. He didn't yell. He didn't scream. He just looked at me and quietly asked, "Who are you, son? Is this you?"

"No sir."

"Are you proud of what you have done here?"

"No sir."

But, there wasn't much else I could say. I knew that I had put others at risk, and that I had quite possibly just undone all of my hard work towards a scholarship. I spent the Sunday morning following my Saturday night DUI with my nieces. I was too embarrassed to leave the house. They didn't know what was going on with me, so they laughed and played with me like things were normal. They begged me, "Watch a movie with us, Uncle Gary."

"All right. What movie?"

"Let's watch *The Lion King*!"

The choice in movie made my day even tougher and more thoughtful. It might sound cheesy to have been stirred so much by a children's movie, but at that point I could not escape the symbolic parallels to my own situation.

In the movie, following a mistaken interpretation of his father's death, the lead character, Simba, flees his home. He goes to the forest and does not want to return to his tribe. Instead, he establishes a carefree existence with few responsibilities.

When an old friend, Nala, arrives and demands that he return to his home, she says something that seemed especially apt to my situation: "You are so much better than what you've become." I knew that I, too, was much better than my recent actions. The Bible talks about "the mouth of babes," being the source of great wisdom. Well, through this cartoon that my niece just happened to be watching, I chose to respond to my mistake proactively. I needed to get myself right, but needed to admit my mistakes to others as well.

When I returned to Rutgers, I spoke openly with the coaches about what happened. I decided not to hide from it or hide it, and started seeing a psychologist for help. I was always taught that ignoring the fact does not change the fact. Ignoring the problem doesn't solve the problem. I didn't think of this as weak. In fact, I did it because I wanted to remain strong. Too many people have misconceptions about not needing help in controlling or overcoming their personal demons. We all need help. Sometimes we can't see the picture because we are in the frame. We need other people to advise us with outside perspectives.

The incident had practical and personal ramifications. Legally, I lost my license for six months. Strange how the inconvenience of asking for rides everywhere makes you consider your actions. I also stopped drinking for a couple months afterward. When I did go out, stone sober, I saw the effects first hand that alcohol had on my good friends. I vowed to be more moderate and careful when I did start drinking again. The reduced partying and the inability to get around were actually blessings in disguise. I renewed my focus on working hard and was forced to cut out all extracurricular activities that weren't positive. My grades improved too. I ended up passing calculus. What else did I have to do but study? Other than study, the answer to that question was: work out. That summer, I busted my tail in the weight room at Rutgers. I only had one year of college remaining, and I had a newfound focus.

On a weekend away from this new mission, I took a trip home for a special occasion. My mom, recently ordained as a reverend, was preaching her first official sermon at Bethel A.M.E. in Lawnside. She was so passionate about this new calling. To see her behind the pulpit, speaking to others with the weight and confidence and loving authority she had so often directed toward her children gave me chills. Perhaps because it was my mother, or because of my recent past, I felt like the sermon was directed right at me. I often felt that way in church. For some reason I connect with words fairly easily. But this Sunday was especially different.

Mom reached into her pockets and pulled out a twenty-dollar bill. She held it up for all to see, even walked down the center isle so people could see it closely, and said, "What is this?"

We all responded enthusiastically, "Money!"

"How much is it worth?"

"Twenty dollars," everyone called out.

Mom pressed on with her point, "And if I asked each of you, after church when we were talking, if you wanted this money, what would you say?

"Yes."

And then, she crumpled the bill up in her hand before saying, "Would you want it now? Now that it is wrinkled and crumpled up?"

"Yes!"

And then she dropped the bill on the ground. She put her foot on it and turned her toes. Then she asked again, "What about now? It is dirty and crumpled and hardly good anymore. Anyone still say they'd want this old thing?"

"Yes!"

"Why?"

"Cause it's money!"

"You are right!" Mom shouted. "The value of this $20 bill doesn't change just because it gets a bit dirty. Just because it does not look as crisp and new as it once did, it is still worth just the same. It is still valuable, and you would still gladly accept it.

"Just like this bill, we are valuable in God's eyes. We may get a bit wrinkled sometimes. We may get the dirt of the world all over us! But we are still valuable to God. How much more are you worth than a piece of paper?"

I was reminded of Nala's line in *The Lion King*. I truly felt that I could be better than I had become. Even though I had started to reform myself, I knew I could still do more. During the altar call, I grew so overwhelmed that I lost control of my emotions. I ended up at the pulpit in tears, felt called there by the fervent belief that God wanted me back. Some people experience a time in their Christian walk when they start doing things their own way. They grow too busy worrying about themselves and worry too little about building the kingdom. I was saved that Sunday, and it changed me. I felt like I had just won a prize. The prize: I got my life back from the devil.

Later, I went back to the team and after one of our workouts I told the team what had happened to me with my recent DUI and how embarrassed I was. But since I was a captain and team MVP I thought by sharing my story I could save someone else from making the same mistake. Sometimes college students, and particularly athletes, feel invincible. But I have learned in life that the wise people learn from other people's mistakes and not their own.

After the interviews that night leading up to the Super Bowl, we all went back to our rooms to change for the evening. This was the only night that we didn't have a curfew so we were planning to go out to dinner. Following dinner, the nightlife in Miami awaited. We couldn't stay out too late. We had to be bright-eyed and ready for the media onslaught the next morning.

That media blitz, known to those in Super Bowl circles as "the formal media session," involved news stations from all over the world. Television networks from Ghana to Germany send reporters to this event. Reporters can range from the serious to the insane. Though all the usual NFL coverage guys from *ESPN*, *Sports Illustrated*, and the big papers are there, the thing that differentiates this interview day from others is the gimmick interviews by people there self-promoting. Of the four thousand reporters there, only some ask insane questions, but insanity is what rules the day. I overheard Rashied Davis from the Bears say about the event, "They (the reporters and crazy celebrity seekers) come out like ants on popsicles."[1] It is nothing less than a circus, but we players are all expected to be professional in the midst of the chaos.

Each player, especially those that are better known, are summoned on this day to stand-alone areas for private interviews. We braced ourselves for ridiculous questions: "How big are your biceps?" "Who do you think is the hottest

[1] Spander, Art. "Colts and Bears Fed to Hungry 4000." *The Telegraph* 01 February 2007, Web 25 April 2011.

guy on your team?" My podium was in the tenth row of the stands at the fifty-yard line. This time, there wasn't a Colts rep to field questions with me. Things started pretty much they way they had ended the previous evening—basic questions about our season. I tried not to use too many clichés, but I cared more immediately about avoiding the Bears' locker room bulletin board. You never want to say something that ends up motivating your opponent.

A reporter asked, "The Colts defense had some really bad moments this year. How did the defense turn it around when everybody counted you guys out?"

"Well, I'm just glad *everybody* doesn't reside in our locker room. We always believed in ourselves and knew that if everybody was accountable and stayed in his gap that we would be successful."

Another question: "I was asking you questions last night, and we got cut off just a bit short. I just had a few more questions if you don't mind. We left off at the end of your junior year. At that point, did you think you had a chance to play in the NFL? What did you think when you went undrafted?"

At this, my mind wandered, and I debated how much detail I ought to get into. I mean, there were reporters here from MTV for the sole point of hitting on players to see if they would respond. I didn't say anything, and just stared off into space thinking to myself.

Going into my senior year, I really only had one goal in mind: graduation. It lingered in the distance as THE goal. When I reached that finish line, I would be the first person in my family to graduate from college. Once accomplished, no one could take that from me.

At the time, pro football was a distant but still desirable option. Nonetheless, I knew I could compete on the field as well as in the classroom. After playing against a Miami team with ten players drafted in the first round that year, and after beating some of those guys on particular plays, I figured I'd be fine at the next level. But I was also aware that my perception wasn't the only factor. Other people had to agree with that assessment and give me a chance. Education was my safest and best bet at the time. After all, my fate in the draft was immediately tied to the success of Rutgers football, and people don't pay much attention to guys on really bad, losing teams.

My senior year, we actually led Miami in the fourth quarter and played quite a few other games where the score was close up until the end. If there are such things as moral victories, we had plenty of them. But tangible victories were few and far between. We won one game and lost eleven. We were competitive and worked hard, but still just didn't have the talent. Looking back, what we were doing was the early grunt work essential for success. Laying the foundation is gritty and dirty stuff, but a couple years later, as Rutgers gained Top Ten rankings with stud running backs Ray Rice and Brian Leonard, we alumni could look back on that achievement with a shared sense of accomplishment.

Despite the team's problems, my personal numbers were good. I finished the season with 131 tackles, a number that put me second in the Big East, just behind Clifton Smith of Syracuse. During our game against the Orange, I kept a close watch on him. He was a good player, but I felt like I was just as good if not better. He drew much more attention, though, because his team happened to be winning. After that season, I had more tackles than the Miami linebackers Jonathan Vilma and DJ Williams, and more than Pittsburgh linebacker Gerald Hayes. These names and numbers mattered to me, since all three of those guys were viewed as potential draft picks. How could I have better stats, on a team with less help beside me, and still get less attention?

At the awards banquet following the season's conclusion, I was invited to speak at the banquet. Every year, one senior was selected to speak, offering some experiences, lessons, and well-wishes for luck in the future. When I prepared for that speech, I considered myself in many ways done with football. I wasn't giving up, but was realistic that I could possibly be done with this game that I loved so much. After speaking, and getting a bit emotional, I was awarded the team's MVP trophy for the second time. Only one other player had ever won two MVP awards at Rutgers, so this was quite an honor. Although we had only won a total of eight games during my college career, those difficulties inspired a new level of intensity and work ethic in me. I have no doubt that those hard years of losing made me a better man today and set me up to approach failure as just another roadblock, and not as the end of a story.

During my senior year, I asked Coach Schiano to help me get me an internship for experience in case professional football didn't pan out. He made a few calls and had a guy lined up in Philadelphia who was willing to have me come work for him. I flirted with immediately taking the job, but I told Coach that I wouldn't be able to live with myself if I didn't at least give the NFL process a full-fledged shot.

With this full-fledged shot in mind, I started looking for agents. Big-name agents did not call. I guess in their eyes I was just one of the many nameless kids who naively pursue a shot at the NFL out of college. I met with a group out of Philly called Premier Sports and Entertainment. They were a small outfit and had a couple of current players in the NFL and the Canadian Football League. Even though Premier offered me little shot of being drafted, and were lukewarm toward me at best, I still wanted to battle for that dream. I began working out on my own without any agent preparing me for Pro-Day.

About a month later I did something a bit aggressive, calling Justin Fine at Premier and telling him that I was ready to sign. He was surprised to hear from me and hesitant about giving me a chance. But he set up a combine of sorts at a workout place called King of Prussia. He wanted to get baseline tests of all my numbers. The workout spot was about an hour-and-a half drive from Rutgers. My numbers there were not off the charts, but they were solid. I had been training at Rutgers with a couple of guys, and occasionally with the entire team. My situation was not ideal. Some of the higher forecasted draft picks worked out with personal trainers and nutritionists. LJ enjoyed some of these perks. Not me. Everyone I worked out with had their own agenda for preparation. I just played catch-as-catch-can, working out with anyone I thought would help push me.

At the time, in addition to the football routine, I was taking two courses. One was an independent research class, which wasn't too heavy. But, in order to hedge my bets, on the off chance that the NFL didn't pan out, I was also taking a finance class. I was working toward enough credits in finance to get a business economics degree. If football wasn't going to be my ticket,

I figured I'd pursue a job on the stock market. I had heard that lots of traders on the floor at Wall Street were former athletes because of the height demands on the floor and the competitive nature of trading stocks.

When the NFL combine passed, and I had not been invited, I looked at the combine numbers from those linebackers who had. My stats were comparable. Rutgers worked up a day for scouts to come visit and watch some of the seniors. Some colleges do this, and players who are highly touted choose that option instead of the combine so they can let their teammates have a shot to get noticed as well. At Rutgers' Pro-Day, LJ was the main event. Because he had so many teams interested, we hoped to use his audience as well. Our plans did not pan out. A couple days before the big day, LJ pulled a hamstring during a workout. Those of us scheduled to work out on the Rutgers Pro-Day got a call—due to LJ's injury, the day was going to be moved back a couple weeks.

Some players were pissed and went out that night to blow off some steam. But those who partied too hard were in for a rude surprise. The workout was originally set for a Friday morning, and that morning we received a call telling us to be at the Rutgers gym at noon for a 1:00 p.m. workout. Talk about short notice! When I got there, I found a motley crew. Some guys were hungover. In addition to current seniors who had just finished playing, some guys who had been cut from Rutgers showed up. How they thought they had a shot I'll never know. When he saw the assortment of guys, and the lack of interest from pro scouts, our strength coach stormed out of the weight room mumbling, "This is embarrassing. I'm not staying for this disgraceful excuse for a Pro-Day."

Because LJ was the main draw, when he pulled out, most of the squads pulled out as well. The only teams that had sent representatives to scout were the more local teams, the Eagles, Giants, Jets, and the Colts. Because we had no preparation, and because no one from Rutgers really knew how to do it, the scouts ran the drills. You know that expression "too many cooks in the kitchen?" Well, we had too many cooks and not enough kitchen space. One particular scout from the Giants must have fancied himself Emeril Lagasse

plus God Almighty. He barked at us and messed up the drills, putting high cones in areas that should have had low cones, setting distances incorrectly, and countless other screw-ups. With this wannabe coach as a distraction, we were all a little hesitant going through drills. How do we do this? What do we do here? These questions were rarely answered completely, which led to some anxiety as we neared the starting point for each.

Everyone was hesitant in starting out these drills, and lucky for me, because my last name started with a B, I was first in line in every drill. We ran forty-yard dashes, something that didn't need to be explained, and I clocked a 4.6, a pretty good time for a middle linebacker in the NFL. We ran a short shuttle, probably my best drill, and wouldn't you know that I slipped the first two times. I still clocked a 4.5, which was pretty good. In turn, the scout from the Colts, a guy named Matt Terpening, must have wanted to see more from me.

"Brackett, I'm going to let you do this one more time. Stop slipping."

"All right, Coach. Thanks!"

For the most part, the scouts worked together and got the same looks. But on a few occasions when they really liked a player they would step up for him and ask to see something again. Without slipping, I took my shuttle time down to 4.2. I knew that was really good for a linebacker. Probably as a result of this success, the rest of the day, Matt took a special interest in me and urged me to fully recover from drill to drill in order to get my best results. The last drills of the day were individual position drills. At the time, when these drills started, there were three linebackers remaining. But the intensity of the drill eventually eliminated the rest of my competition. Ron Simone, a Rutgers linebacker, cramped up and stopped doing the drill. So then there were two.

Next, we did a drill that simulated dropping into coverage and catching the football. The scout from the Giants was supposed to be the "quarterback," but his arm was terrible. The balls were going everywhere and were rarely even remotely catchable. Far be it from us, tired and expecting him to miss the throw anyway, to miss one of the few shots we had at the ball. In the middle of this drill, Mitch Davis, the only other linebacker left beside me, grew so exhausted he walked off the field, saying, "I can't do this, man. This is ridiculous."

Ridiculous? I'll tell you what is ridiculous: to have the chance of a lifetime and let one person deter you from your goal. I didn't care what self-obsessed scout from the Giants said to me about my value. I knew what I was capable of better than he did and wasn't about to let him convince me that I was somehow limited.

After Mitch left, the scout now turned his full attention to me. "Are you going to quit like the other two?" he asked. And mumbling just loud enough for me to hear, he added. "I knew it was a waste of time coming to Rutgers for this."

Again Matt stepped in, and although he couldn't throw, he let me catch my breath and put me through the final three drills as a conditioning test. He expressed pleasure in how I performed.

"You did well today," he told me. "You are on the Colts' radar. I'm not making you any promises, but there's a chance we would be interested in bringing you in. I'd like to give you a Wonderlic test when we get back into the offices."

I lit up! It no longer mattered that most of the thirty-two NFL teams hadn't shown up for the workout. All I needed was one team to like me, and I had my one team—the Indianapolis Colts.

13

The day of the draft brought with it excitement and anxiety. LJ had eventually had his Pro-Day; twenty or so teams came out to see him. When I say they came to see him, I mean him and only him. The same rag-tag group of players from that first, haphazard Pro-Day came back thinking, now there will be some new teams to see me work out. Wrong! We were all wrong. Charlie Weiss, then the Offensive Coordinator for the New England Patriots, was the spokesman for the group, and as he got things rolling he said to the group of players standing around LJ, "Sorry, guys. We are on a tight schedule and only have enough time to work out LJ."

The other teams followed suit. We were all upset, but because of LJ's notoriety and the Rutgers Pro-Day, we had at least gotten a partial chance. Meanwhile, LJ's stock was rising fast. At the combine, he had blown it up. Teams drooled over this six-foot-four, 265-pound tight end who ran a 4.5 forty-yard dash. Interested teams had also surely heard that LJ worked extremely hard. There was little question he would make it to the league.

The weekend of the draft, LJ hosted a draft party at his house for his friends and family. He had an outside chance of going in the first round, which was an achievement that also brought financial rewards. Signing bonuses for those in the first round are significantly higher than those in later rounds. We waited anxiously as names were called, but the Philadelphia Eagles, the team that had flirted with taking LJ early, traded picks so they could pick a defensive end first. Their choice had played at Miami. The 'Canes were the measuring stick for talent at the time. The Eagles did end up drafting LJ in the second round with the sixty-first overall pick. We were all stoked. We were like a band of brothers, and when one made it we all felt good. DeWayne Thompson, who was also hoping to be drafted, and a few other teammates were there rooting for LJ on that opening round day. Those of us with an outside shot of being drafted all knew that the next day would shape the rest of our lives.

The second day of the draft holds rounds four through seven. These are the less glamorous rounds, but much of the talent around the league comes from that second day of the draft. I had spoken with Matt Terpening from the Colts a week earlier. They were the only team that had shown any interest in me. My big hope was the Colt's fifth round pick. Actually, they had two picks in the fifth round, but I figured I'd be the second pick if I went. That day I watched alone for all my nerves, but I was in constant contact with my agent Justin.

"Gary, you watching?" he asked.

"Of course I'm watching. This feels like it is taking forever. I didn't know until this year that teams had five minutes to pick. I just wish some of them would stop using all that time and hurry up. I'm glad in these later rounds they don't have quite as long to choose."

With their first pick of the fifth round, the Colts selected Robert Mathis. At the time, he was a little known player out of Alabama A&M so not many people had seen him play. This next pick was where my agents had told me I might land. When Keyon Whiteside's name scrolled across the screen as the second fifth round pick for Indy, I was frustrated. He had played at the University of Tennessee, and Rutgers had played them that year, so I had seen him play. I considered him a good player, but I thought I was better or at least as good. The Colts didn't have any picks in the last round, so if I didn't go with their sixth-round pick I figured I wouldn't be drafted at all. That round drew more frustration. The team that I knew was my one and only shot chose Cato June from Michigan. At the time, I was in disbelief. This guy, later my best friend, was on this day a source of intense frustration. After a few minutes of staring at the TV in dazed disbelief, I started to think about my other options. I wasn't yet willing to give up on my dream, but when I figured out that the draft wasn't happening for me, I called Coach Schiano to see if he would check back on that internship. Was it still on the table?

Toward the end of the seventh round my phone rang. When I saw that number was blocked from showing up on the caller ID, I wondered...could this be a team calling to let me know they were going to draft me?

"Hello?"

"Yes, is Gary Brackett there?"

"Yes," hoping the caller didn't hear the anxiety in my voice, "this is him."

"I'm calling you from the Eagles and I wanted to let you know...I wanted to let you know..."

It wasn't a team on the phone. It was my boy Dewayne. We both cracked up at how anxious I was.

"Have you gotten any calls, Brack?"

"No, what about you?"

"Nothing."

"What the hell?"

"I don't know. But with some of those guys that were drafted, guys we have seen play and competed against, I know we are both good enough to get a shot."

Right after I hung up, Matt from the Colts did call. At first, I was hesitant. As he said his name, I racked my brain for some memory of his voice. Sounded like the same guy, but I didn't want to get fooled again.

"Gary, I'm going to be honest with you. We think you are going to go undrafted. That said, we want to be the first in line to chat with you when the draft is over."

"That sounds great, Matt. I just want a shot."

After the draft, the Colts did contact my agent. We agreed to terms of a contract, and the signing bonus was a whopping two thousand bucks. The money didn't matter to me. Whatever I was getting paid, I was going to be paid to play a sport I loved, and I was just excited to get a chance. Matt gave me some reminders about things to bring to camp. I needed to go shopping.

The next morning, I had a bright idea for my 9:30 a.m. class. I thought that I would impress people if I came in to class with the hat of my new team. Especially impressive would be if the Colts somehow magically sent me a hat overnight, so I could have it first thing in the morning. When I arrived at the mall, the hat store was closed. I pleaded with the guy at the store,

"Come on, man. I just found out last night that I am going to get a tryout with the Colts. I want to wear a hat to class to show off."

"We aren't supposed to be open until 9:00."

"Yeah, I feel you. But I need this! This class's professor didn't think I had a chance, and now I want to rub it in a bit."

"OK, OK. I'll sell you the hat."

"Thanks! I appreciate it."

My arrival in class was a bit tardy, but when I entered, everyone in the room immediately stood and started applauding. If you have never seen a black kid blush, you should have been in Hickman Hall Room 204 that day. After class, folks gathered around and asked for autographs, gave me pats on the back and words of congratulations. This feeling of support was just what I needed for the journey to come. After all, an invitation to try out was one thing. Making the team was quite another.

When I arrived in Indianapolis, I was scared out of my mind. The Colts had some great players, guys I'd watched in college: Peyton Manning, Edgerrin James, and Marvin Harrison. Reggie Wayne was arguably making a push to take over as the first-option wide receiver, which is really saying something, given how good Harrison was. The defense had Dwight Freeney, David Thornton, Walt Harris, and Rob Morris at my position—MIKE, also known as middle linebacker.

As I drove onto the grounds, signs around the Colts facility directed all players to head to the locker room. From there, we were directed to the cafeteria where they had set up a makeshift office with about ten desks to sign in players. This was, after all, a job, so paperwork dominated the first day. They asked for birth certificates and social security cards. As I filled out those forms, it felt like I was shaking like a leaf. Maybe I really was shaking like a leaf. But you would shake too if your childhood dream was in the midst of coming true.

We met our linebacker coach, Mike Murphy, a 5'8", fifty-something-year-old, white male. He helped install our defense. The Colts had invited four other new linebackers, making a total of five rookies. Competition, sure, but these numbers were good in my mind. How else does a fast learner show off his skills than through a little competition?

My optimism was not blind. I held no illusions about the chances of the average rookie free agent. Many teams hire free agents after the draft and call them camp bodies. Because of the rigors of an NFL training camp, teams start the season with about eighty-five guys even though they know some of those guys won't stick. The active roster in the season has only fifty-three players and about five more earn a spot on roster. In other words, those five are inactive but can be activated given injuries. Those last five get paid a great deal less. Those players sure to start often get more chances to rest during the summer months so they don't burn out or get injured during the pre-season. Even though everyone knew I was a long shot, people treated me very respectfully. The first time I met Coach Dungy, he welcomed me by name, "Gary, I'm Coach Dungy. So glad you are here. You know, you remind me a bit of Nate Webster, who I coached in Tampa."

I'm not sure what my response was, though I am sure it was filled with stuttering. As he spoke, all I could think was *YOU ARE TONY DUNGY! AND YOU KNOW MY NAME! HOW DO YOU KNOW MY NAME?*

Coach Schiano had compared me to Nate Webster as well, and I felt like two coaches making the same comparison probably meant that the similarities were real. In the midst of such praise, I felt motivated to prove that I belonged, at least on the practice squad. The only problem was that I was fourth on the depth chart, which didn't warrant a lot of playing time. I saw an opportunity on the second day to get some snaps, even at a position I typically didn't play. The Colts were light at SAM, or strong-side linebacker, since two players were looking for a rest. The starter, Marcus Washington, had just undergone surgery and was sitting out mini-camp. Coach Murphy wondered aloud to himself, "SAM...SAM, who can I put at SAM?"

Standing next to him, I spoke up, "Coach, I can play SAM."

"You know SAM?"

Hell, we only had three plays in so far. I had memorized those inside and out. Plus, if you knew how to play linebacker you could play any of the positions. He put me in, and I spent the rest of my first NFL camp as a SAM linebacker.

This worked well at camp, but it left me with about zero chance to make the team. I just didn't have the right build for this position. Usually, the SAM linebacker was the biggest linebacker out of the bunch. The SAM is responsible for playing man-to-man on the opposing team's tight end, or dropping into short zone protection on pass plays. I just didn't have the size for it. But my chances wouldn't be limited to defense only. Just like at Rutgers, I earned my jersey on special teams. The next practice offered that chance.

In the NFL, squads film their special teams to review after practice. I wanted to get on film to get noticed. But I wasn't on the starting special teams group or even listed as one of the few subs. My only option was to start at the bottom, to work my way into the group that ran down the field to give the return squad a look. One of the guys from the D-Line had body language I could read like a book. He had no interest in running down the field, especially for what he viewed as no real reason or opportunity. But, as Thomas Edison once said, "Opportunity is missed by most people because it is dressed in overalls and looks like work." So, I offered to relieve him of his obligation to run.

I said, "Hey, Hicks, you want me to run down for you?"

"You wanna run down for me? Why in the world would you want to do that?"

"It don't matter. Just toss me your beanie." I put the beanie, a cloth covering that covers your helmet and helps differentiate offensive players from defensive ones in practice, and thought: *this could be it. Now or never.* During the first drill the ball was kicked off and I flew down the field before the guy assigned to block me even turned around. I ran right to the ball carrier and made the play. Our special team coach yelled out in response, "Where the hell did he come from?"

When everyone else was silent, I responded, "R1, Coach." (R1 is the first person on the line to the far right.)

Darnell Thompson was the guy responsible for blocking me. After I made the first play, Darnell started talking a bit to me

"Ok, you wanna go for real, 58? Well, bring it. You ain't gonna make me look bad out here."

"I'm just trying to give a look. No confrontation necessary."

As I reassured him, I knew that my sole purpose and best shot was to make him look bad. We kicked off again. For a second time I hustled down the field, but this time he was ready for me. He got in position to block me, and approached surely expecting a collision. At the last minute I made a spin move, he whiffed again, and I ran down the field to make the tackle. I knew that the coaches had noticed, but so had Darnell, and not in a good way. After that play he walked over to me and told me, "You better watch yourself. I'm going to be out to get you if you keep practicing like that."

I couldn't care less what he thought. Practicing like that was what was going to get me noticed. He was my direct competition at the time. He was second string and a starter on special teams. I'd have to battle against guys like that to make the team.

After that weekend mini-camp, I went back to Rutgers to finish up with my classes. My time on campus was one of excitement. It felt like things were really going right for me. To share my excitement, and to pick his brain, I went in to chat with Coach Schiano about the mini-camp.

"How did it go, Gary?"

"Everyone was nice. The facilities were amazing, but I gotta be honest, Coach, I felt like a fan most of the time. I mean, watching the NFL's top offense go to work and operate like a machine? It was awesome."

"Well," Coach asked, "how do you think you did?"

"I think I did well on special teams. Hopefully, if I'm lucky, I could make the practice squad or something."

"Whoa whoa whoa, Gary! Practice squad? Is that all you aspire to?"

"Well, I mean I want to play, but I guess I got to wait my turn."

He urged me to think differently about things. He argued that one of the main reasons guys don't make it in the league is that they don't expect to. He said at that level everyone has to prepare like the starter, "Don't program your mind to be on the practice squad. Program your mind to start. Didn't you learn that lesson here in college? Changing the way you think will change the way you prepare and go about your business. Forget about the names on the back of the jerseys. Think of each player as a number and a position instead of Edgerrin James "Rookie of the Year, two-time rushing champ." He is just RB #32. Respect others, but don't idolize them. That way you don't have to compete against gods, just mortals."

I remembered the conversation I'd had with Wesley Robertson a couple years earlier when I'd aimed for a scholarship rather than starting. Here I was again getting complacent and limiting my goals. We shouldn't just reach for the lower bar, or the one right in front of us. We should shoot higher than we even think possible.

Supporting this realization was Coach Schiano's authority on the subject. He had been the secondary coach for the Chicago Bears, so he knew what life was like in the NFL. He had actually set up our training and conditioning program to be similar to what he had seen at the highest level. I listened closely to this ally of mine that had been there and knew what he was talking about. *I do need to change the way I am thinking. I am going to prepare for the job I want.*

Upon graduation, I enjoyed a big celebration at my house in New Jersey. We had much to celebrate, so the party was something of a three for one. I had graduated college on May 22. My twenty-third birthday was on May 23, and I had just gotten my first job as a member of the Colts. Only thing was, one of those—the last part of that celebratory equation—still needed to be proven.

The party must have included close to three hundred people in my back-yard. Everyone was excited, but some of them had misconceptions about my new life. When guys get picked up on an NFL team, their friends and family expect instant millionaires. The fact is I had never been so broke in my life. The signing bonus of $2,000 was reduced to $1,200 after taxes. We were getting paid to work out, but that only amounted to about $200 a week after taxes. Housing was paid for, but that was about it. I had the lowest body fat in my life but not because of my extreme hard work; I was so skinny due to a lack of funds. Every night, dinner brought another Subway sandwich. Every lunch brought an even cheaper variety of sandwich—peanut butter and jelly. Every once in a while I splurged and bought some Laura's Lean Meat to make burgers on the George Foreman grill I brought from college.

This weight loss didn't adversely affect the way the coaches felt about me. During training camp I met with my position coach. "You raised a few eyebrows at mini-camp," he said. "While I admire you for filling in at SAM, I don't think that position is best for you."

We both laughed. We had a running joke about how short we both were, but he brought us back to business, "Coach Dungy believes that if a kid can play he can play, and your height will not keep him from making the team. We want you to move back to MIKE backer, where you are a more natural fit. You'll start at third string behind Rob Morris, who you know has been our three-year starter, and Keyon Whiteside."

I was thrilled I would be third, but was almost more excited when he told me that I'd been moved up to the second kickoff team. At that camp, every day felt more demanding than the last. My body was exhausted. Our typical schedule was as follows:

7:00am – Up and eating breakfast early enough so your stomach can settle before the first practice
9:00am – 11:00am – Practice
12:00pm – Lunch
2:30pm – Film / meetings with position coaches

*3:30pm – 5:30pm – Second practice of the day, finishing with
sprints and conditioning
6:00pm – Dinner
7:00pm – 10:30pm – Film / meetings with position coaches*

After this long day, you go to sleep quickly so you can be as rested as possible for the next day.

In the second week of camp, Rob Morris went down with a knee injury. Keyon and I both thought we would move up a spot, but instead they moved over the second string SAM linebacker, Jim Nelson, to start at MIKE linebacker. This was our introduction to the first rule in the NFL—the best people always play first, even if it means they play out of position.

Leading up to the first pre-season game, the coaches told us what quarters we could expect to play. I was told that I would play special teams in the second half and maybe linebacker in the fourth quarter. Either way, I was hyped. On the short drive to Chicago, all I could think about was the game. I had only seen one NFL game live. As a young kid I'd scalped a ticket to an Eagles game, but I was so high up in the stands I might have well been watching ants.

We won the toss and deferred the kickoff to the second half. This meant that Chicago received the ball first. They had a nice thirteen-play drive down the field. On the last play, just before they attempted a field goal, Jim Nelson ran off the field holding his hand and signaled for the doctors. Whatever his diagnosis, it looked like coaches were going to have no choice but to go to the young guns. Our defensive coordinator, Ron Meeks, gathered the linebackers coaches and said, "Jim is down, who do you want?"

After a couple of obscenities, Coach Meeks said, "You sure? OK."

Keyon and I watched this scene, and heard these words. We both knew the rankings. He was up next. But for some reason Coach Meeks shouted, "Brackett, you're in."

"What?"

"You're in, genius," he chimed.

I grabbed my helmet and started getting ready, stretching and loosening up. I had warmed up early in the game, but I wanted to make sure I was ready. It wasn't the time for me to worry about Keyon. We were cool off the field, but on the field I knew they were only keeping a few of us. Things were going to be tense during the next few weeks.

In retrospect, the reason I got the nod over Keyon was because I was a natural MIKE, capable of taking calls from the sideline and echoing them in the huddle. I had experience calling plays and then going on to do my job. Keyon played weak side in college and wasn't accustomed to thinking that much on the field. He was more of a reactionary player than play-caller. Keyon had made a few mistakes, and the veteran defensive line always gave a long sigh when he took snaps with the first team in practice. To be fair, I had an advantage because the defense was very similar to what we ran in college. These advantages that I had enjoyed over the previous weeks did nothing for my nerves on this day, however. On the first play, I was crazy nervous, but I called it, "Under Smash."

Some of the D-line replied, "Huh?"

I barked back, "Under Smash. Let's Go. Ready?"

"BREAK!"

"Under Smash" was a blitz in which I would come off the defensive end and get to the QB. It wasn't an effective blitz. Chicago threw a quick pass for a short gain, but with my first NFL hit under my belt my nerves started to settle. I played the rest of the first half and third quarter before Keyon got some snaps. During my time on the field, I played pretty well. I had some tackles and also did a good job on special teams.

When we got back to practice the next week, Jim's Xrays were back. He had broken his hand and would be out a couple weeks. This time the coaches had no one else to put in front of us. I would remain the starter for the rest of the pre-season. This gave me a ton of reps to show the coaches that I could play. I couldn't wait for a home game. And our second pre-season game fulfilled my anticipation.

Waiting in the tunnel for the defensive starters to be announced before that game, my heart raced to the frenzied chants of the Indianapolis crowd.

I was so fired up! When the announcer finally boomed from the field's center speakers, "And, at Middle Linebacker, a rookie from Rutgers...Gary Brackett," I sprinted out of the tunnel to the roar of 58,000 people. It was like I was exploding from a thunderous new life as an NFL player.

We played the Seattle Seahawks, who at the time had Shaun Alexander. He was one of the better running backs in the league, so when I dove in the open field to tackle him, I felt something like a superhero. In that game I had two quarterback hurries and forced two incompletions. It wasn't a great game, but I certainly hadn't embarrassed myself. Finally my childhood dream was playing out in real life. To date, the experience remains my most memorable moment of a long athletic career. It was absolutely surreal.

It was tempting after a couple of pre-season starts to think that I was a lock to make the team. But I continually cautioned myself—*not so fast*. In college, you're just competing against the people on your team for playing time. But in the NFL you are also competing against the players from thirty-two other teams. If a linebacker somewhere else in the league doesn't make his squad, and the Colts like that guy more than me, they very easily bring him in.

After the first few pre-season games, I did make it up to the final cuts. If I made it through this last round of cuts, I would be officially on the squad for the year. I would be a Colt. Needless to say, the ordeal was nerve wracking! The coaches told us, "Final cuts tomorrow, guys. Remember, we don't keep the best players; we keep the best unit. We want the best team, not the best collection of players." But how could I know where I fit into that equation? Was I part of that best unit? The night of the final cuts I went to my hotel room.

At the time, I was sharing it with Dontae Booker, a big defensive lineman from Auburn. Booker was about six-foot-four, 295 pounds and had a very country demeanor. He had bought a dog the last two weeks of camp, saying it reminded him of home. If you have never lived in a hotel room with a guy that large and a dog, you cannot imagine how ready I was to get out of that room.

Booker and I sat around the entire Sunday playing video games and waiting for the phone to ring. It was a two-room suite with a living room so I was in the living room, and he was in the bedroom with the TV. Neither of us had a clue where we stood in the pecking order, and when the phone rang we both just looked at each other. After the second ring, I took the bullet: "I'll get it…Hello?"

"Gary, this is Steve Champlin from the Colts."

"Yes, Mr. Champlin."

We all knew that this was the guy who would call and tell you that the coach wanted to see you. After that, it was presumed that your time was done.

He said, "How are you doing?"

Well, I wasn't doing so well. My heart dropped because my worst fears had come true. I said, "I've been better."

"Well, I don't know about that. We are calling for Dontae. You are safe. You made it."

I made it! I didn't want to show my excitement in front of Dontae because I knew what had just happened to him, so I waited till he left to go hand in his playbook. Once he left, at that exact moment, I cried tears of joy. I called home.

"Mom and Dad, are you both on the phone?"

"Yes?"

I was surprised Dad had answered and sounded so good, but I was wrapped up in my own moment.

"I made it!"

"You made it?" Mom said. "What does that mean? You have a contract and spot on the team?"

"I will soon!"

Dad said, "We are so proud of you."

This was the second time in my life I'd heard those words from my father. He didn't hand them out easily, preferring instead to teach us toughness and the survival skills he viewed as necessary in a world all too hard to navigate. When he did express his pride, I felt as if I just might burst with my own.

That Wednesday night, since all of our families were slated to arrive in Miami on Thursday, Cato, Reggie Wayne, and I went out to eat at one of the best steak and seafood places on South Beach—Prime 112. Eating out would not only give us a chance to relax over good food, it would also give us a chance to take a peek at the Miami strip. We were staying in Fort Lauderdale, about a forty-minute drive to the restaurant and surrounding nightlife.

With the team curfew, we would not normally take the chance of getting stuck in traffic and somehow missing curfew, but Reggie eliminated those concerns. He had played for the University of Miami in college and lived in Miami during the off-season. As a result, he knew Miami like the back of his hand. No traffic jams for us. If in a bind, Reggie could navigate back streets and shortcuts like he was dodging would-be tacklers on the field.

On our way to dinner, we stopped at his condo to get a few things and to see the place. So many professional athletes live elsewhere during off-season and we never get to see each other's houses. I was also struck by how funny it was that, here we were as the Indy Colts, and Reggie was coming "home" to Miami to get some things for the first time in a while. Many players live as transplants. I could understand his desire to stay rooted in Miami. His condo was located in the middle of the downtown and had an amazing view of the Miami skyline. We teased him about the exclusivity of the place.

"Dang, Reggie, security guards everywhere. Guess they have to make sure we belong."

"Yeah, yeah. I've been to y'all's places. You ain't exactly slumming it."

We arrived at the restaurant to find a who's who of the NFL. Our teammates, Bears players, announcers, and media types were all there. This was the place to be in Miami.

The menu was a mix of Surf-n-Turf, steak and seafood of all sorts. Since we can't get the freshest seafood in Indianapolis, the middle of America, I figured I'd try more of the Surf this evening.

"Yeah, can we get the lobster claws as appetizers please?"

As we ordered, we started to reflect on the season. Cato started us down this particular road: "Can ya'll believe, after all those years of losing in the playoffs, we are finally here? Look around this room, man. This is the big event."

Reggie responded, "The strange thing is, I don't know that this team is any more talented than the teams in years before. That 2005 team could have made this kind of run. Bill Polian (our team president) claimed that team was the best team he's seen since he's been here in Indy. We were a certainly a better team than Pittsburgh all year. Can't believe they came into our house and beat us."

"Don't even get me started," I said. "I would have gone down in the history books if Nick Harper hadn't been tripped up by Ben Roethlisberger."

Cato echoed my sentiments. "I know, right, the great Jerome Bettis—The Bus—and you stick him hard enough to knock the ball out on the goal line as they were about to score."

Reggie added, "I guess it wasn't meant to be. To get here, you have to be good and lucky."

"I think those losses in the years before 2006 just made us more determined, set the stage for this year. As far as this year goes," I said, "I'm just glad we got the defense turned around. The announcers were killing us during those last four games of the season—*The Colts' defense can't tackle anyone*—and though I knew they were wrong, it sure is nice to prove it on the field."

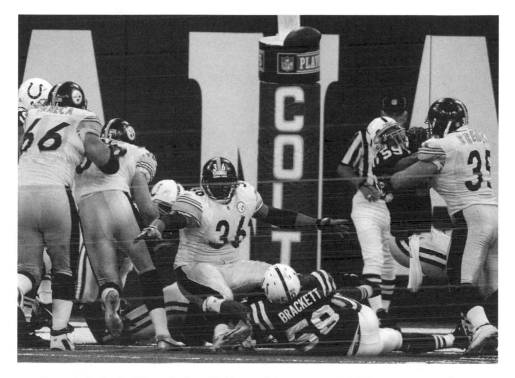

Reggie joked, "I'm glad ya'll figured it out FINALLY, too. But I do wonder, how did the worst defensive team in the regular season become the Steel Curtain D in the playoffs?"

This was a good question. We had some struggles in the regular season, that is for sure, but our defense didn't struggle early in the season. We actually started off the year on fire. We won our first nine games—enough for all of the experts to start talking about whether or not we'd be able to keep the momentum. Only one team had every finished a season undefeated, the 1973 Miami Dolphins, and after every season when the last undefeated team loses, that Dolphins team always pops open a bottle of champagne to celebrate their continued monopoly on perfection. When our perfect season ended in week ten, it seemed like our ability to win concluded as well. We lost four of our next seven games.

"During the losing streak," Cato said, "I think everyone for the most part did their job during the early portions of each loss. Then once a few bad runs or missed assignments came along, everyone started street-balling, running around with no structure. We are back to winning again because we are back to playing Gap defense and believing that all of the other players out there on the field can cover their assignments."

I think the lowest moment during that stretch, other than the sheer fact of losing four games in a row, was when Jacksonville ran for 375 yards against us and beat the hell out of us 44–7."

I agreed. "They manhandled us. I mean, they are always tough cause they're in our division and everything, but the D laid an egg during that one. Bob Kravitz, the beat writer for the *Indianapolis Star*, wrote that the only reason the Jags didn't run for 500 yards was because the end zone kept getting in the way. I was most embarrassed because I knew how good we could be."

"You remember how smartly Coach Dungy handled that?" Cato asked me.

"Yeah, he was calm and everything, but he told us plainly that our performance recently had been unacceptable, that we needed to do better. He knew what the rumblings had been in the locker room: *We are too vanilla as a defense. We need to change things up and trick teams.* But he didn't buy it, and we went in the completely opposite direction."

Coach Dungy's strategy didn't change with our struggles. He'd always believed that teams didn't win with tricks. Teams win with fundamentals. So while some of our defense wanted more complicated schemes and coverages, he actually took away plays from the game plan.

"Guys, we are going to play two coverages. I don't want ya'll thinking about us. I want you focused on outplaying our opponent. You just have to do what you are capable of doing and do it more often. Let's do what we do better than they do what they do. In every NFL game there are at least thirty plays where the offense and defense both know what is going to happen. The team that executes assignments the best will be the victor."

Reggie didn't want us taking too much credit. "What do you guys think of the media saying so much about Bob Sanders? Does he make that much difference?

Bob was arguably our best player on defense. He stood 5'9" but was an absolute wrecking ball on the field.

I responded, "I don't think it is that simple. Bob is Bob. He is without question a great player, and he increases our chances of winning. But our improvements over the playoffs have been team-wide. I think moving Rob Morris to the starting squad helped us just as much." I continued, "Even though Rob is playing SAM linebacker right now, it helps me so much out there to have someone else who knows the coverages and can help orchestrate our defensive setup before snaps. He lightened my load mentally, which frees me up to be a better and more reactionary player."

"I still can't believe how well y'all played in the first playoff game against Kansas City," Reggie raved.

"I know," I said, "it ain't like Larry Johnson is a joke or anything. For us to struggle so much against the run towards the end of the year, and then for us to play like that against maybe the best running back in the league, that was big."

Reggie said, "Without question, from my perspective, Johnson is one of the best backs in the league. For you all to hold him to forty yards…"

"Thirty-two yards," Cato corrected.

"Crazy," I said, "and the next two games were just as great. We held the Baltimore Ravens to just six points, and that comeback against New England came, after all, largely from a defensive play. Reggie, you almost gave it away with that near fumble on your last drive."

"Yeah, but I didn't," Reggie said, "I don't know if I'd give ya'll more credit for that win. After all, we were down 21–3 early on and had to score a good bit to make up. But I don't have many complaints considering where we are sitting. Marlin Jackson's interception of Tom Brady's pass to seal it at 38–34 was truly clutch. Credit another one to defense."

"You all just make sure you put some points on the board, Reggie."

After our meal and chat, we headed back to the hotel, aware that we had to leave early the next morning for practice. It was tempting to go out to see the nightlife in South Beach, but the hotel was the best choice at the time. Celebrations were pending, but we had some work to do first.

The night before the big game I slept restlessly. So at 8:00 a.m., I decided to stop trying. I rolled out of bed. Super Bowl Sunday! And this time, I wouldn't be watching it at someone's house. I wouldn't be wondering what it would be like to be in it. I'd be the entertainment for the nation. I checked the news for a few minutes before hopping in the shower.

Our 9:00 a.m. scheduled breakfast was to be followed immediately by a 9:30 a.m. meeting. One thing I don't particular like about night games, you have to go to another meeting and then you have to sit around all day and wait too many hours, often until 4:00 p.m., before catching a bus for the stadium.

Others wait in the room even longer than me. There are three busses to the game, two of which arrive about three hours before kickoff. I usually go on the earliest bus and am normally joined by players with injuries needing treatment before the game. After four pre-season games, sixteen regular season games, and three more playoff games, the Indianapolis Colts were now heading into our twenty-fourth game of the season. It probably goes without saying that the first bus can be crowded—more players have nicks and bruises than those who don't.

The bus ride to the stadium is always, despite what the movies often depict, very calm. This day was no different. I needed my energy, and thought of this period of quiet reflection as the great calm before the storm. Muhammad Ali once remarked that, "The fight is won or lost far away from witnesses; behind the lines, in the gym, and out there on the road, long before I dance under those lights." Who am I to disagree with the great champ? I always know where I stand in the game before it even starts, and can base that knowledge on one question: how well have I prepared? I constantly review my notes regarding the opponent's schemes and packages (always focusing on that team's "money down" tendencies) right up until running through that tunnel. We make our money on every down, but none matter so much to the success of a defense as third downs. Can our D get the opponent's offense off the field and our offense back on?

On Super Bowl Sunday, the bus arrived at the stadium, and we got off and headed to the locker room. I traveled early in order to get in some time with Bryant Baugh. He is one of our best trainers so his time is in high demand. We started with the Colts the same year and are the same age. He has been waiting exactly as long as I have for this day. We looked knowingly at each other and had to say absolutely nothing about the significance of the moment.

I go through a number of different stretches and massages pre-game. I focus particularly on the elbow injury I sustained against the Patriots in the AFC championship. It remains sore, but is not nearly bad enough to keep me off the field this Sunday. I go through an ultra-sound and massage to get it warmed up. As the treatment of my elbow finishes, the remainder of the team arrives. All of us are fairly tired of talking about the game. How much can we talk about one game we haven't even played in? How much can we analyze an opponent? Get us on the field finally!

The most striking thing during warm-ups on the field is the number of cameras. I'm amazed at how many TV stations are here. I had no idea this number of stations even existed, but I told myself to stay focused.

No distractions, Gary. Stay focused. This is just a regular game. Yeah right, my common sense interrupts, *a regular season game that the whole world happens to be watching.*

After heading back into the locker room before warming up, we always say a prayer as a defense and then go off for some time to ourselves before

Coach Dungy calls us together for the Lord's Prayer.

Even on this unusual day, I observed my usual routine. I went to my locker and took a knee. I wanted to address those to whom I owe this day, my mother, father, and brother. I knew that they were in heaven looking down on me, but I still wished they could be watching from the fifty-yard line with the rest of my family and friends.

Lord, thank you for another day on this earth. I pray that you watch over both teams tonight as we go into battle. I'm grateful that you brought me through so many tough times in my life and have positioned me to be here to play for a chance at the title. I thank you for giving me my mother and my father for over twenty years of my life. I know that some people go their whole lives without knowing their parents. I thank you for the special bonds that I have with this team, Lord God, and these men that you put in my life. I ask that you continually work with me and build me up so that I can do more, not for my own glory but for yours. Lord God, in Jesus' name I pray. Amen.

Mom, Dad, and Greg, you got the best seats in the house. I know you're in heaven looking down. We are here now as a team. We just have to finish the deal. Enjoy the show. As I wondered again about those cameras and the crowd that waited, I wondered what Dad would have done had he been alive for this. He hated crowds....

After I made the Colt's roster, I enjoyed all the newness of playing this sport as a pro. One night that season, I was out with Cato after a Monday Night Football victory. While we were enjoying the evening, my sister called about five times in a row. When I finally did feel the vibration of the phone, I looked at the screen and saw *Five Missed Calls*. I immediately wondered what was wrong. As I answered, it took my sister a few seconds to communicate clearly. She was crying too hysterically to speak, so I anticipated that something was wrong.

She said, "It's Dad."

"What about Dad?"

"He's, I can't even say it. He's just died. He's gone."

My body recognized the weight of her words perhaps more quickly than my mind. I felt an instant chill go through my body as I stood beside the pool tables in the club. Time froze, or at least slowed beyond recognition. It must have taken ten minutes for the bottle I was holding to fall to the floor, shattering just like my childhood upon this news.

Cato was startled by the falling bottle, but when he looked to me for an explanation and saw my face, he knew something was wrong.

"You all right, Gee?"

No response.

"Gary. You OK?"

"I."

"I."

"That was my sister. My dad is dead."

Saying it. Labeling Dad as such, somehow made it more real, and I shed my first tear in years. Cato's surprise lasted just a few seconds. He turned around, said goodbye, preparing politely for us to leave by saying good-bye to folks out with us. Then he said, "Come on, man. Let me get you home."

It was one of the eeriest rides of my life. Any other time we would be jamming to music or cracking jokes on somebody. Not this time. We passed the time in silence, which made more room for my mind to spin. What could ever possibly prepare you for such a loss? As Cato dropped me off, he spoke for the first time since we'd left the club. He turned, breathed deeply, and said, "You have to stay strong for your family, bro. I'm here if you need me. But you have to be there for the rest of them. They look up to you."

The claim that someone is "there for you," is perhaps the most overused one in the world. But, coming from Cato, I knew he meant it.

That night I didn't sleep. I thought of Dad. Stories he told me. Times he had made me so mad I couldn't think. How he had always been on time for everything. So many memories...my first job was delivering newspapers. The months of September and October were particularly pleasant, but then the weather starts to turn nasty in New Jersey. When it grew colder and the days shorter, I started to like that first job less and less. Dad insisted that I keep working, but he helped me deliver them during the coldest weeks. These two elements of his character carried me so far: he demanded I finish what I started, but would help me if I needed it to set me up for future success.

The next day I woke up early to head to the complex and meet with Coach Dungy. When I sat in his office he read the sorrow in my face.

"Coach, I just got word that my father passed."

"Oh, Gary. I'm so sorry to hear that. Is your family still in New Jersey?"

"Yeah."

"When are you heading back?"

I hadn't known what the rules were regarding things like this. How would

I have known? But I didn't think that I'd be allowed to leave so quickly. I'd anticipated just going back for the wake, but that expectation failed to account for the type of man Coach Dungy was.

I asked, "Are you all right with me leaving?"

"You have to go home as soon as possible."

He'd always preached family first, and now I got to see that he really meant it, "Take as much time as you need. Some things in life are bigger than football. You are welcome back here when everything is finished."

When I landed, my brother Grant was at the airport to pick me up. In the car with him were Torrey Brooks and his brother, Ali. They had lost their father in high school in a motorcycle accident and knew how much we'd need a support system. As we pulled up to our house I counted six cars visiting. This was fairly standard for a family grieving; just close family and friends coming by the house to pay their respects, offering their condolences with a hug and their quiet presence.

When I went inside, I chatted quietly with those in the living area before gently knocking on my mother's door. She was alone inside the room lying on the bed crying. When she got up to greet me I gave her a huge hug, "Mom, I'm sorry. I love you."

"Gary, I'm glad you're here. What am I going to do? I can't even mourn your father I am so stressed about all the stuff I have to arrange. I have to pick out flowers, a casket, a suit and shoes."

"We'll get it done, Mom. I'm here to help."

"Can you do something for me now? Can you pick out a suit and shoes and take it up to the funeral home? I don't have that in me."

"Sure. I got it."

As I glanced through his closet, so many of the items looked familiar. I didn't recognize some of the shirts and shoes though. I hadn't seen Dad much over the previous years. His PTSD and claustrophobia had kept him from coming to any of the Rutgers games. The only times I'd seen him had been when I'd been able to get home briefly over weekends. My senior year at Rutgers I'd only seen him infrequently. At the time, I was busy trying to graduate and make it into the league, and often spent my weekends flying to Indy for workouts with the team. Still, I felt guilty about not seeing him more often. I wished I wasn't new to these new clothes. Even on those times when I was home, Dad's chain smoking drove me out of the room. I took it for granted that he'd be here for a long time. Now that he was gone, I wished I'd spent some more time in those smoke-filled rooms.

On one of those occasions when we did share a hazy room, he told me that he was dying. I didn't want to hear it, so I got up and tried to leave. "Gary, sit down. With you just graduating, and heading out to Indy, you need to know something. I am proud of you. But I'm not going to be here forever. You are going to be the man of the house. Your mother will need you when I'm gone."

"Let's just stop talking about this please."

At the time, I just listened and wanted it to be over, but this was Dad's version of the passing of the guard. Well, now this change in the guard was no longer hypothetical. Now it was real.

As I drove to the funeral home alone and considered these new levels of responsibility, it hit me in a whole new way that I had lost my father. *Here I am in the parking lot of Carl Miller's funeral home. Taking clothes for my father.* With this thought, I exploded into a flurry of tears and anger, pounding on the steering wheel.

"Why? Why? How is this fair?"

It didn't take long for God to answer me. His words came in the form of a song by Smokie Norful. It was the first time I had heard it, but the lyrics seemed especially meant for me at that moment. The song asks for God's help at a specifically trying time.

Not a second
Or another minute
Not an hour
Or another day
But as this moment with my arms outstretched

I need you to make a way
As you've done so many times before
Through a window or an open door
I stretch my hands to you
Come rescue me
I need you...
Right away
I need you now
I need you now
I need you now
I need you now.

Like the songwriter, I needed God more than ever at that moment. As the song played my rage subsided. I realized that God was reassuring me that he was with me. This realization gave me a strength I'd lacked moments before. With this new resilience, I took a deep breath and handed over my father's funeral clothes, just like my mom had requested. When the funeral director received the shoes he asked if I wanted to see him.

"Excuse me... Yes. I am here to give you some clothes for Granville Brackett."

"Yes, Mr. Brackett, but do you want to see the body in these clothes? It will only take me a few minutes to prepare."

I froze and didn't know how to respond. *No, I don't want to see my father like this.* But another part of me pushed back. This would be the last time I'd have a moment with him alone.

"Yes, I want to see him."

This marked the first time I'd seen a dead body since my best friend Rashaun's funeral, and I had some things to say to Dad as the funeral director left the room to give me some privacy:

"Hey Dad. I miss you. I'm sorry we didn't have more time together. Thanks for everything you did. I'll always owe you."

The day of the service, everyone wore their black suits and dresses and the family was escorted by the funeral directors from our house to the service. Because of the size of my family and all of my dad's family and friends, the funeral crowd overflowed into the basement of the Mt. Pisgah Church.

The service was nice. Readings from Psalms assured us that in these times, "Help comes from the Lord/The maker of Heaven and Earth." My Aunt Lori sang "Precious Lord." She sang that first verse,

> *Precious Lord, take my hand*
> *Lead me on, let me stand*
> *I'm tired, I'm weak, I'm lone*
> *Through the storm, through the night*
> *Lead me on to the light*
> *Take my hand precious Lord, lead me home*

As she sang those words, I thought about their dual meaning. We children and friends of Dad needed something upon which to lean. But Dad, too, must have longed for comfort as he was escorted "on to the light...(and) home."

Though our sorrows were great, we'd had some warning that this might be coming for a while. Dad had suffered one big heart attack in the mid 90s that prevented him from working and converted the hardcore Marine into a stay-at-home father.

That stay-at-home father was a new sort of man, not the same dad we grew up with. When he'd returned from his long stint at the VA Hospital, after the episode with Greg, he was clearly a changed man. This change occurred, not coincidentally, the same time he accepted Jesus Christ as his personal savior. But his newfound religiosity and changed ways could not reverse the harm he'd done to his health. His heart condition slowly deteriorated. Years of smoking had also drained him of energy. Our phone calls, so long a ritual after every Rutgers game, had over the years grown shorter and shorter. The last couple of games, when I actually called, my mom answered and told me that my dad wasn't feeling well enough to talk. Afterward, that father-son ritual became a mother-son one instead.

GRANVILLE L
BRACKETT SR
SSGT US MARINE CORPS
MAY 5 1946 ✝ OCT 14 2003
SANDRA E   HIS WIFE
JUL 15 1952   FEB 20 2004

After the funeral, we departed to the burial grounds. Since Dad was a marine we headed toward Arneytown, N.J., which was a burial ground for men who had served their country. When we arrived and the body was brought out of the hearse, the service men there began playing "Taps." In the military, the nature of your salute depends on your rank. A sergeant in the marines receives a twenty-one-gun salute. Seven soldiers each fire three times. The first round that went off—"Fire"— sent chills through my body. The second was even more violent. As I stood next to my mother, I reminded myself to stay strong for her. I knew that she would know if I was crying despite my jet-black glasses meant to hide any tears. When the third order was given—"Fire!"—I couldn't help but feel as if it felt final. I lost control.

This man who had demanded so much from me, demanded I live up to my own best, was gone. I had lost him forever. A single teardrop rolled out of my right eye and down my cheek, my own final salute to this man who'd taught me to be a man myself. At the end of the service the military representatives folded up the flag crisply. They put the bullets in the middle and handed the bundle to my mom. She would not have it for long.

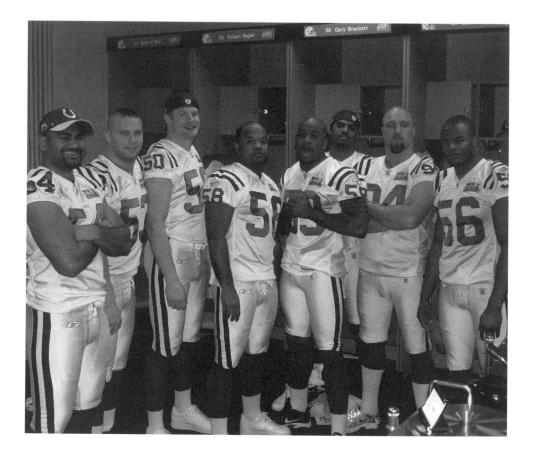

I think often of my dad, every day in fact, but sitting here, in this locker room, before an event I know that he'd have been so excited about was too much. Memories of him just flooded my consciousness, one after the other. But as I sat thinking I was stirred from my thoughts.

"Gary?"

"Hey, Mr. Irsay."

"How does it feel to finally be here? Finally here at the big game?"

"It is a dream."

"Well, good luck out there. Win one for Indy."

"I'm gonna do my best!"

After my dad's funeral, I returned to Indy to rejoin the team. Mr. Irsay was one of the few people who had noticed my absence. My position coach had also missed me, and Coach Dungy offered his condolences once again, and my linebacker crew supported me in my return. Cato and David Thornton continually made sure that I was OK. Their support made us even closer as friends. But Mr. Irsay's words to me at our next game upon my return, really stuck with me. He said, "I am so sorry for your loss. I am praying for you and your family. Know that the Colts support you."

The comfort that I received during this process from the entire Indianapolis Colts family made me perpetually indebted. To have the owner of a team personally offer sympathy is a far cry from the Rutgers AD who continually called me the wrong name.

This team doesn't pay lip service to family; they act on the values that they profess.

That first season, we, as a team, ended our season as we too often did, losing in the AFC Championship game to the New England Patriots. When I returned home, I had a thicker wallet than when I'd left. Because of the success we had going to the AFC Championship game, and the rookie performance pool, I took home almost $350,000 my first year in the league. Not bad for one year removed from college.

After my father's funeral, I wanted to do something with Mom that made her know I cared. Like so many pro athletes, I always vowed that if I ever made it to the NFL, I would buy my mom a house. With this new money from my rookie year, I intended to make good on that promise. So, during the off-season we went house shopping together. Eventually we found an area where she would build what she called her "dream home." Mom's dream was my dream, so I made the down payment. The house even had a little basement I planned to use when I returned to visit in the off-season.

Despite my desire to help, Mom was doing pretty well on her own. She was a busy woman. An ordained reverend, she often traveled to different churches to speak as a guest preacher. The day after we went house shopping together was a Sunday and I went to hear her preach. As I watched this usually mild and reserved woman, I was amazed. It was as if the robe somehow hit a switch and she was transformed.

This quiet woman became, in front of my eyes, a powerful motivational speaker. She spoke about my father and how much she missed him. She spoke about her kids and how in life when things got tough you had to press on. She spoke about how, as a fan going to our basketball games, she would always notice the coach's actions during tight games. He stood up, put his hands together, and called for the full court press. Life is the same way. When things get harder, we just have to turn up our energy levels as well. Just as our press tried to prevent the other team from scoring, sometimes you have to outwork the devil to keep him from doing the same thing. All we have to do is, according to her, "bend our knees, roll up our sleeves, and press forward to the kingdom of heaven."

That February, my mother and I spent countless hours shopping for the new house we were about to build, but our focus was briefly interrupted by what was supposed to be a routine operation. Due to some reproductive system issues, Mom was going to have a hysterectomy. This would supposedly improve her quality of life, but there was one problem. Mom had suffered a stroke previously, so she was on a medication to help with her blood flow. The doctor told her to get off the medication in preparation for the surgery; if she stayed on it, her blood would be too thin and wouldn't clot.

My sister and her best friend, Courtney, accompanied my mom to the hospital for the operation. I was going to go visit her before I took back off to go to Indianapolis. By the time I arrived at the hospital, Mom had been under for a few hours and was expected to be in surgery for a couple more. I asked my sister if she wanted to go get a bite to eat while we waited. She agreed. When we came back the nurse approached us with a frantic look on her face. "The doctor needs to talk to you," she said.

We went into the waiting room, and Gwendolyn picked up the phone. Almost as soon as she placed the receiver to her ear, her face dropped. Afterward she said that she could tell by the tone of the doctor's voice, something had gone terribly wrong. I grabbed the phone from my sister and identified myself.

"Well, Mr. Brackett. We experienced some complications during the surgery. Your mother had a stroke in recovery."

"What does that mean?"

"The stroke shut down most of the function in her brain. We'll monitor her and keep you abreast of what is going on."

I felt terribly upset and sure they had done something wrong. What had happened? Why wouldn't this stupid doctor speak to us face to face? As we waited to receive any updates, we got on the phone and called family members, telling them what had happened and to come quickly to the hospital. We didn't get to see Mom until about 1:30 in the morning. After seeing how bad she was, we agreed that we should take rounds staying with her at the hospital until she recovered.

I did not have complete faith in the doctors who were treating my mom. I was angry at what I felt must have been their mistakes and certainly didn't feel as if they were speaking honestly to us. I called my agents at the time, Justin Fine and Michael Steinberg, and asked if they knew of any ways to help. They made countless calls on my behalf and couldn't find anyone that would take my mother under these circumstances. All of the medical folks stressed to me that it was important that my mom remained in a stable position.

This scene was different for me than my father's situation. I wasn't around for the end of his life, so I had no idea of the complexities that were involved in the hospital. Justin and Mike were there to field my calls and answer some of the questions that the doctors would not. At the time, they were the most sophisticated people I knew, and they gave me insight into what I should be doing at the hospital. For about two days I drove back and forth to the hospital just to watch my mother lie there in a coma. It felt like each time I went in the hospital, she died all over again. I couldn't imagine my mother's life continuing under these circumstances. My mother was vital and full of life. She wouldn't have wanted to linger aimlessly as a coma patient.

One night driving home from the hospital, I started praying to God, asking Him, "What are you trying to get me to see here? What do you want from me?" I was frustrated and angered. Almost as an answer straight from the heavens, the song "Everywhere I Am" by Jaheim played over my car's speakers:

> *(Just when) I'm inches away from losing my mind*
> *(That's when) I swear sometime*
> *(I hear your voice inside my head) and it feels like you're*
> *(Everywhere, everywhere I am)*
> *(Just when) the walls are closing in on my world....*
> *(Clear as day inside my head) and it's obvious you're*
> *(Everywhere, everywhere I am)*
> *....If god is in the sprit world talking to my heart*

Then for an angel I know it can be hard
You are my guardian and I know you're still playing your part
(I know you are) Just on the other side but always in my life
No need to just believe I know you're here with me
I'm reaching out my hand and to the promised land
To feel your presence when I need strength

The song confirmed my feelings. Mom was no longer here with us. She had become an angel and was waiting for us to allow her to go on to the spiritual world to be with my father. When sitting with loved ones during their time in the hospital, for some reason, I often think of funny television episodes or jokes. Maybe I am trying to laugh to keep from crying, but as I thought of Mom's last months I was strangely reminded of an episode from *Seinfeld* where his father was sick and had been rushed to the hospital. The family would come to visit and found their dad hooked up to the heart rate monitor. When his wife left the room, his heart rate would go down. When she came back in, his heart rate went back up. She left again and his heart rate dipped in response. In his puzzled kind of way, Seinfeld deduced that his mom was in fact killing his father. Her mere presence in the room automatically increased his father's heart rate.

But when Seinfeld approached his father with his finding, his dad refuted his logic, saying, "That is the most ridiculous thing I've ever heard. The reason my heartbeat rises dramatically when your mother enters the room isn't because she is killing me but rather because she gives me life." When they were separated, he didn't feel whole without his better half.

It made perfect sense to me this is what happened to my mother. When my father passed, I would at times walk past Mom's room. Though the door was usually closed, I could hear her weeping to herself. The pain that she felt was unbearable. Her lifelong friend had passed, and she was hurting.

The fact that my mother was still alive was something of a myth. She wasn't breathing on her own and was solely being kept alive from the breathing machine. It was easy to guess that she wouldn't want this, but because she died without a living will, we children would have to make the tough decision. In those days, I questioned God a great deal. What had I done to deserve all of this? What did Mom do to deserve such suffering? I remembered something Mom had once said to me when I complained about not getting help from the high school coach in looking for scholarships,

"Gary," she'd said, "we cannot change the cards that life deals us. We can only change how we play our hand. We cannot change where we were born or who our parents are. We cannot change anything in the past. All you can do is move forward and focus on things that affect your future."

As I remembered those words about moving forward into the future with the cards I'd been dealt, I knew that I had the strength to do what needed to be done. We scheduled a family meeting, at which everyone tiptoed around the elephant in the room. We made small talk until I spoke up, saying, "I thank everyone for your continued support. It's been a very rough couple of days, and we have some very important decisions to make. Knowing Mom, we all know that she would never have wanted to be kept alive by a machine."

The room was filled with tears and everyone knew what had to happen, but no one wanted to make the decision. I remembered my father's words, and knew I had to step up. What gave me peace was knowledge of my mother's faith. Since we as a family shared it, we knew that if God was going to step in to make a miracle he wouldn't need a breathing machine to make it happen.

Everyone hugged each other and comforted one another for support. My Grandma was in attendance and she made a very poignant observation. She had known about our plans of building a new home and had gone to a couple of stores with my mom to pick out light fixtures and paint colors. She noticed that often my mom spoke about the house's gold statue and immaculate entrance. Maybe Mom, even without knowing it, was already preparing for a home away from this physical one. Maybe the home my mom referred to was in fact her spiritual home. We needed to enable her to go home to be with Dad and the Lord.

Together as a family, we finally decided to stop the medical devices keeping our mother alive. She died like anyone would want to die, free of pain and with her children by her side. The hymn at Mom's funeral reflected our feelings about her final release. It was joyful indeed that she was able to reunite with her husband and meet her maker:

> *Joys are flowing like a river,*
> *Since the Comforter has come;*
> *He abides with us forever,*
> *Makes the trusting heart His home.*
> *Blessed quietness, holy quietness—*
> *What assurance in my soul!*
> *On the stormy sea He speaks peace to me.*
> *How the billows cease to roll!*

"Two minutes, Coach!" Jon Torine, our strength coach, shouted these words to Coach Dungy, the cue for his pre-game speech.

Coach's speech was just what we needed at the time. If he had tried to pump us up, we might have gone over the edge. Instead, he urged us to stay within ourselves. "Guys, we don't need any superhuman efforts from anyone tonight. None of you have to play out of your minds. All we have to do, is do what we do, and we have to do what we do better than the Bears do what they do. That is all this game requires. If we do that, we will be successful and we will make our mark in history."

On our way out to the tunnel, we kept encouraging each other—

"Do what you do!"

"Do what we do!"

The tunnel to the field felt too long, and as we came near the end we could feel the sixty-degree evening blowing outside and see the rain in the lights high above the stadium. Those minutes felt like they were conspiring against us and keeping us from actually setting foot on the field. Let's just play already!

This anticipation was not quickly remedied. The pre-game ceremonies were extended as Billy Joel sang the national anthem. He was not the only celebrity in attendance that caused the crowd to roar. The loudest was per-haps the Air Force Thunderbirds, whose flyover rattled the stadium and threw chills down my spine. Peyton Manning, Adam Viniteri, and I walked out to mid-field as team captains. We shook hands with the Bears representatives, Brian Urchaler, Rex Grossman, and Thomas Jones.

"Gentlemen, let's have a good clean game. This side of the coin is heads. This side is tails. Peyton, you call it in the air."

"Heads."

"You called heads. It's tails. Bears, what do you want to do?"

"We'll receive."

Looks like the defense would get this party started. I ran to the sidelines pumping up the defense.

"Get ready! Let's go. Let's set the tone."

We prepared ourselves to get things started right. Unfortunately, things went haywire before we ever saw the field as a unit. When Adam kicked off, Devin Hester, out of the University of Miami, and possibly the most electric return guy in the business at the time, took the kickoff all the way "to the house" for a touchdown. Longest return in Super Bowl history at our expense.

All week in practice the coaches had debated back and forth—should we kick to him or not? You have two options with a guy like that…avoid him altogether, or go at him and execute coverage perfectly. We chose the latter option, and found out quickly that execution was easier said than done. So right out of the gate, 7–0 Bears. Not exactly the start we wanted in the biggest game of our lives. The only positive was that we had all game to make up for that mistake.

I focused on this fact, drawing upon some of my brother's words he'd once used to encourage our high school squad when he was a senior,

"Come on, guys! This is a long ball game. No one thought it would be easy. They hit us first. How we respond is up to us."

How I wished Greg was here to see this…

"Hello? Wake up! Wake up, bro!"

I rubbed my eyes and looked at the clock, the voice came from the phone again, "Get up, Gary! It's time to go kick some butt!"

"Not yet, Greg. It's an away game. Out here in California we are three hours behind you all. You must have read the schedule wrong."

"Hah hah! My bad, lil' bro. But, hey, gotta wake up sometime. Play well today. You know I'm proud of you. As much as you looked up to me as a kid, I look up to you like that now. So wipe the sleep out of your eyes and get your day started. Love you, bro."

"Aight. I'm up. I'll talk to you later."

This emotional phone call from across the country would hardly have come from the Greg I'd grown up with. He would never have been so honest and open about his feelings. But since his diagnosis about five years prior, he had been different. He said that he realized the need to treat loved ones affectionately.

"You know how people bring flowers to a funeral? Well, what do the dead get out of those? I want to give people flowers—metaphorical ones—while I'm still here."

Though Greg and I had been especially close throughout our childhood, our bond had grown even more after he got out of jail. He'd served three years for the shooting with the Williams boys, and when he emerged from jail he was a new man. He started his own business and got his head screwed on straight.

Football had always been, and continued to be, the lifeblood of our bond. Whereas Granville and Grant both loved basketball, Greg and I were drawn to those Friday night lights in high school. I had idolized him. It was Greg who the coaches compared me to; in his shadow I had grown, and out of his shadow I'd eventually emerged as my own Brackett on the field. This connection, and my memories of him as unstoppable in the family yard, made his illness harder to bear.

In the summer of 2003, Greg had checked into the emergency room complaining of stomach pain. A host of tests revealed that he had Stage 1, T-cell Neuroblastoma Leukemia. Well, Greg didn't back down and won the first round. Before Mom's death, he had officially beaten the cancer. We were optimistic.

Who knows the ways of the human body, however? After Mom's death, he went in for a routine check-up to find that the cancer had returned. Like an unstoppable army advancing through his blood stream, the disease started to seek out new territory. Quickly, Greg was in need of bone marrow transplants. The doctors asked him if he had any siblings. The entire family dutifully made the trip to the hospital in New Brunswick to get tested to see if we matched as a donor. The hospital was located near my apartment during my senior year and was very close to Rutgers' downtown campus.

As I drove to the hospital to get tested, I was torn by a mixture of nostalgia and guilt. How would I have gotten to college without Greg's example? I had no doubt in my mind about who the donor would be. I was in good shape from my constant workouts, and could probably withstand the strain more than the others. But my fitness wasn't what would clinch it. Greg and I were practically twins. When he turned 21, I turned 21. We shared so much in common, why not blood types?

The results came back and my suspicions were confirmed. The doctors couldn't narrow the time frame for me, but they told me that sometime in the next six weeks they'd be calling me to come in and donate.

"This process will not be too painful, but you will need time afterward to recover. Your energy will be severely affected."

As I waited for the news on the transplant, I reported back for training camp in 2004. Coach Dungy greeted me with a big hug and words of welcome. He knew that I'd just lost my mother, and of course knew about Dad as well.

"I'm getting through it, Coach, but I've just had some more bad news. My brother has been diagnosed with cancer. The doctors tell me that I'm his best match as a bone marrow donor."

"When it rains, it pours, huh? You know, I just lost my father to cancer last year. You need to do whatever you can to help."

"Well, I plan on donating, but I don't know when they'll call me in for it. There are some issues with my brother's insurance, and they have to pre-approve the procedure."

"Whatever happens, the Colts will support you when you need to go. Your family comes first."

Coach was a man of few words, so when he offered these subtle words of comfort, he put my mind at ease.

I got the call in May of 2004. It was the same month of mini-camp.

"It's time, Mr. Brackett. You need to come in quickly. Your brother can't wait any longer."

I felt guilty because I was torn about going. I was fighting for a starting job, but I had the chance to help my brother fight for something far more important, his life. I went home to prepare for the process. It was fairly intense and invasive.

Perhaps the worst part was the three days prior to the actual transfusion process. On those days, I took Neopregen shots to build up my white cell count. White blood cells respond to infection, so those shots essentially mimicked an illness. I felt truly sick, like the flu but worse. While waiting for the shots to do their work, I spent three days in a row at the hospital hooked into an IV. A machine removed blood from my left arm, filtered it to separate the cells and to extract certain things. After that, the red blood cells remaining were pumped back into the right arm. After my own treatments, I walked with my brother to his.

During this time in the hospital, I came to view cancer as a great equalizer. It hits everyone, rich and poor, white and black, the educated and dropouts. The worst was the way families looked in those hallways. No one seems to speak out loud in hospitals, as if by whispering you can somehow hide from the fates. Faces look heavier, like the weight of these battles drains outward expressions as much as the internal strength. The experience was emotional and formative. I vowed that if I ever had the financial capacity, I'd do something to help families going through such things.

When the machine was finished with me, I made my way back to Indy. The team was in the middle of mini-camps, a draining experience in their own right. The doctors had told me that after this transfusion I'd immediately be ready for resuming my "regular" lifestyle. I guess that the NFL mini-camps are not included under the banner "regular." Two practices a day, with all that running and installing new plays, is apparently more than the average body goes through.

When I arrived at the Colts complex, I felt anxious to prove myself. After all, this was only my second year in the league, and I felt obligated to prove that my previous year's success wasn't a fluke. We were in organized-team-activities mode. We practiced just once a day and did more team meetings type of stuff. The trainers knew what I'd been through and asked if I felt up for practice.

"Of course. The docs cleared me."

But as soon as we started revving up a bit in warm-ups, I began to feel lightheaded. Since this was only my second year, I didn't want to make excuses. Instead, I just fought through it. But, for the first couple days, I wasn't myself physically. My reflexes felt just a bit dulled, yet the physical toll wasn't the worst of it. After losing my mother and father in a nine-month time span, the vicious cycle was beginning anew with my big brother. My body was heavy and so was my heart.

Thankfully, the coaches gave me some time to get it right. Since I wasn't expected to be the starter, the spotlight wasn't shining directly on me just yet. My goal at that point was to be on the team. I kept thinking of a joke heard around the locker room, "You know what those letters stand for? NFL? Not For Long! We all got short careers in this league."

With everything that I had going on, the joke didn't feel too funny. It was starting to ring more and more true as my doubts grew about what I was doing here. Can I do this? Should I be doing this right now? Shouldn't I be back with my family?

My doubts about my choice were exacerbated by phone calls updating me on Greg's status. I heard from him pretty rarely, but knew from my siblings he wasn't doing well. During that next season, as I was eating breakfast one morning, my phone rang. When I saw the 732 area code I knew it had something to do with Greg.

"Hello?"

"Gary." His voice was raspy and soft due to infections from the chemo-therapy.

"It's Greg. I'm dying."

Tears immediately streamed from my eyes and I walked away from the table, "Don't say that, man. We have to remain positive."

"I've lost eighty pounds during this thing. I weighed two hundred when this started and am down to 120. I just want you to know, before it happens, that I'm proud of you."

"I'm sorry I'm not there for you right now."

"Hey, your life doesn't stop for this. You gotta keep on it. I'm going to miss seeing you play, little bro. And, don't apologize. There's nothing you can do for me now. Thanks for giving me a chance. Don't beat yourself up for what you are doing. Don't quit working hard, man. You gotta succeed for all of us."

Greg was indeed doing poorly, but he held on for a while longer. At the time of that call he was suffering from a severe response to the transfusion. The way chemotherapy works strikes me as crazy. In essence, it is poison whose goal is the death of your body's cells. After killing those cells, Greg would need my blood to jump-start his system again. We had known the risk of the bone marrow transplant, and now our fears were validated. Greg suffered what is known as Graph vs. Host disease. Essentially, his immune system rejected my cells. So, now, he not only had this illness in his blood-stream; the blood itself was poison for his system. He suffered several infec-tions and eventually he lost his voice and couldn't speak.

In that morning conversation, Greg continued to dissuade me from giv-ing up on football to come home for his sake. My sister Gwen had warned him that I was talking of coming home. I thought that money and the dream of football paled in comparison to my need to support my family,

"That is the dumbest thing I've ever heard," he told me. "You'd be doing Mom, Dad, and yourself a disservice. You just promise me you'll be a role model for those kids of mine."

"I got you, Greg. I got you."

As I promised him I'd look out for his kids, I glanced at the clock. "Ahh... Greg, we have a meeting that started five minutes ago. I've got to go or they're going to fine the hell out of me. I'll call you after practice."

"OK. We'll talk later."

In my rush to the meeting I had to wipe the tears from my eyes. I snuck in without being detected, eager to avoid what I had heard were thousand-dollar fines for being late. For the rest of the day, the words "I'm dying," haunted me. I needed to see my brother.

After practice, when I called Greg, his girlfriend answered. She told me that he was doing OK, even though he often woke up with nightmares or convulsions that caused foam to bubble out of his mouth. I didn't believe her when she called him "OK," but respected her for being there with him. This respect was magnified by the fact that my brother didn't always treat her like she deserved, and that even in the midst of that she stood by him throughout his whole ordeal. She drove him to this hospital, woke up in the night to tend to him, and generally helped him through an impossible time.

I finally snuck home around November after a win. Usually, when we won, we got Monday and Tuesday off. I walked into the hospital fairly blind as to what exactly was happening to Greg. My family couldn't explain things over the phone adequately, and Greg had instructed the doctors not to call me. He didn't want me worrying about him. Because I was not on the list, they wouldn't share any of his information with me when I called. When I arrived at the hospital they had a harder time avoiding me.

The nurse actually responded with surprise when she saw me: "Greg! What are you doing out of bed."

"Ha ha...I am Gary, Greg's younger brother."

"Oh, Gary! Your brother has told the whole floor about his brother who plays with the Colts. He brags all day about his baby brother in the NFL and how Indy is going to win the Super Bowl. Even better, he plans on being there!"

On the flight home, I had tried to prepare myself for Greg appearing very sick. The reality was much worse than I'd expected. He was actually convulsing when I walked into the room, covered in bedsores because he hadn't been able to move regularly. I hadn't seen him since he lost all that weight. It was too much, and I broke down seeing him like that. His girlfriend was surprised to see me,

"Gary! How did you get home? We just watched the game on TV yesterday!"

"We have Monday and Tuesday off. How long has he been like this?"

"A while. And to make matters worse, last week they had to put in a catheter. He can't even get out of the bed these days to go to the bathroom."

Greg was heavily medicated, but he roused when Tonya greeted me. As he got his bearings and looked at me he started to cough. He tried to speak, but the words didn't come. I moved in closer to make out what he was trying to say, but I couldn't. Tonya didn't need words to understand what was happening though, as constant a presence as she had been.

"He has to use the bathroom. He can't get out of the bed. He needs help. They just let him go on himself."

I lifted him up out of the bed and helped my brother, my idol, go to the bathroom. I've run sprints until I couldn't breath. I've injured hips and hands and ankles. I've experienced full-speed collisions with some of the biggest and baddest men on the planet. None of those things compared. This was by far the heaviest weight I'd lifted in my life.

I stayed as long as I could. While there, I received bad reports from the doctors. Apparently, Greg had already passed away two times, but they had been able to revive him. They did not expect positive results.

I thanked the doctor for speaking with me and went to the hotel. For the next few months, my mind was in Indianapolis, but my heart was back in that hospital with Greg.

After the season was over, I again visited the hospital, and Greg was in a little better shape. He had begun to work with a machine that helped you understand some of the words he was saying. He was conscious more frequently, though still mostly out of it. At times, the pain prevented him from even opening his eyes.

This glimmer of hope we'd felt was soon lost. The next round of infection led the doctors to make a prediction they had so far avoided: *Greg only has a few days left.* The numbness from my parents' deaths lingered within me still; yet here again came death, marching on inevitably.

I thought of my brother's life, the richness of our lives, and how much more my life had been enriched by Greg's presence in it. I didn't know how much more I could take of this. How much can anyone stand, and from what can we draw strength? The Brackett clan all gathered at the hospital. Friends and family all there to share this pain together. The doctor came in and told us he was sorry, but that Greg was only being kept alive by a breathing machine. My oldest niece, Jasmine, Greg's oldest daughter, was in the room as we listened to the doctor's words. We had been in this same situation just months before with Mom. Someone has to decide, but we all knew what was inevitable.

Jasmine stood up and spoke about her relationship with her dad. "I don't want to see him like this anymore. I don't want him to be in this kind of pain. I don't want to wake up every day overwhelmed by the fact that I have to watch my dad suffer like this. It needs to be over. He'd want it over."

We knew what had to be done. Without even mentioning it, we called the doctor back in and told him to remove the life support. The doctor nodded, and invited family in to be with Greg during those last moments.

19

The crowd roared and I looked up. Interception for Chicago—their day just got better. Looks like the defense was on the field for the first time. We needed to make a stand, so I put my memories aside to make room for the present.

Man we got some work to do. After Hester's opening return, all of a sudden we were down 7–0. The offense marched down for a drive but ended up giving Chicago good field position after Peyton threw an interception. So we had two levels of pressure as a defense that instantly hit us. First, there was little room for error, as we were already behind. But with this reality on our minds, we were forced onto the field on short notice and with a short field to defend. The sense of urgency for players increases dramatically and things feel more frantic after our offense suffers a turnover.

Compounding our concerns, on the other side of the ball, we faced some formidable foes clicking on all cylinders. Rex Grossman had struggled a bit during the season but had turned it around during the postseason. They had a talented back in Thomas Jones, who had rushed for over 1,200 yards that year. At receiver, they were led by Muhsin Muhammad, an older and savvy player who knew how to come up with a big play. Bernard Berrian was enjoying a breakout season at receiver as well, and provided another player we absolutely had to keep our eyes on. If we wanted our team to stay in the game, we had to tighten up and hold Chicago on this first possession.

Their first play of the game was a seven-yard pass, not the best start for us. We were already on our heels. The next play was a Power, and I recognized the formation immediately from watching how the opposite guard was lining up and standing. I attacked the line of scrimmage and tackled Thomas Jones to prevent any gain. This set up the first third down of the game for the Bears. We would have to win our fair share of third downs if we wanted to win the game.

At the snap, Rex dropped back but quickly had to scramble when Mathis and Freeney pressured him. In the face of this pressure, he threw an incomplete pass. We ran off the field pumping our fists. Momentum is a fickle thing in football, and we wanted to make sure the Bears didn't seize too much early. This stop was important.

After the punt, our offense ran a couple short passes and handoffs. On third down, Peyton and Reggie struck. Peyton dropped back and scrambled around in the backfield. Just before he was tackled, he launched the ball down the field and found a wide-open Reggie Wayne. Reggie grabbed it sure-handedly, racing fifty-three yards for the touchdown. We were back in business. That we fumbled the extra point didn't dampen our enthusiasm.

Now that we'd scored, we had a decision to make. Devin Hester had hurt us right off the bat. Would we kick to him again? This time we squib kicked. Essentially, we kicked it short so Hester couldn't catch it. We gave up a few yards right off the bat to prevent the big play. This decision worked out even better for us than we could have hoped. On the kick, Robert Mathis came down the field like a bullet, putting his helmet squarely into the football. The up back that caught the ball fumbled, and Tyjuan Hagler recovered. Our offense got to take the field again in great field position. We all knew how much we owed Mathis for this swing in momentum. Earlier in the year, when our kickoff team was struggling, he requested a spot with that squad to shore it up. Established players rarely make such a request, but it had certainly paid dividends in this circumstance. Now we held the momentum card!

It didn't last. On a handoff immediately thereafter, we fumbled and the Bears recovered. Yet another sudden call for the defense to respond to. This time we didn't fare as well. Thomas Jones broke a long run of fifty-six yards to put the Bears in great field position. The next play, Muhammad caught a nifty little pass across the middle for a touchdown. Not even eleven minutes into the game, and we were down 14–6. The defense felt as if we'd just been hit in the mouth.

Our offense stalled in their answering drive, which put the pressure back on our defense. Cedric Benson, a bruising and talented running back in his rookie year after being picked fourth overall, came in for Chicago. On his first play after entering the game he received two things: a cutback handoff from Rex Grossman, and a hit courtesy of Bob Sanders. We recovered the resulting fumble for good field position again. We would not allow another first down for nearly two quarters.

This time, the Bears kept our offense out of the end zone, but we still got some points from an Adam Vinatieri field goal. We'd known from his days kicking against us when he played for the Patriots that he was clutch. Good to have him on our side now! This kick was the first of his three field goals in the game.

After Dominic Rhodes scored a touchdown for us on a short run toward the end of the second quarter, we went back into the locker room leading the Super Bowl 16–14. Both teams had three turnovers, a sign that the rain was influencing the game. But even with the weather slowing us down, our offense had moved the ball well up and down the field. If we just kept doing what we were doing, we'd be in good shape. We felt good about how we'd played. With our 257 yards of total offense and the Bears 95 yards—half of which came on the one big run by Thomas Jones—we felt we could do two things: move the ball and stop them from moving the ball.

During halftime, we refueled with oranges and Gatorade. The crowd listened to Prince play "Purple Rain" in the rain as we prepared to listen to our coaches' halftime adjustments. But, because we had played pretty well, we didn't have much to correct. Coach Meeks stressed to keep doing what we were doing: "Keep playing hard, men, and I promise you, you will spend the rest of your days as champions."

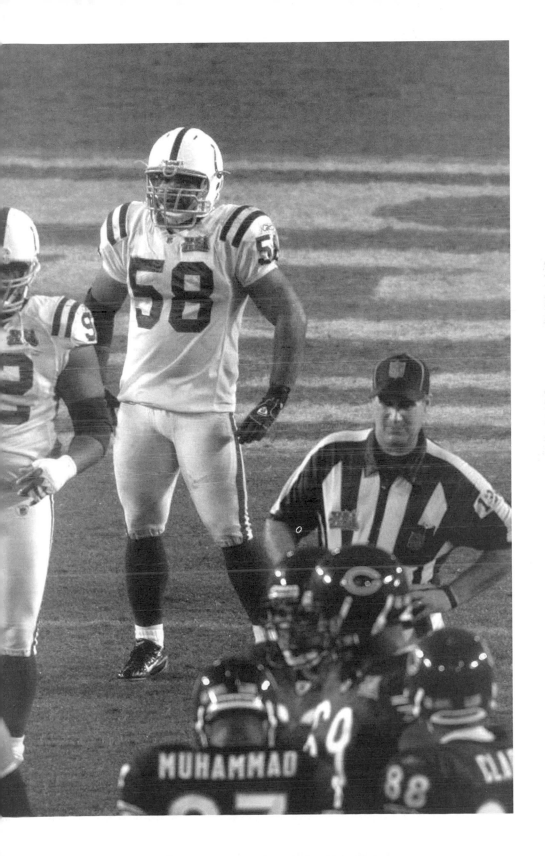

After meeting with position groups, Coach Dungy pulled the team together and shared with us a famous quote he used from Tom Moore, our offensive coordinator. *The winner of this game is going to be whoever plays the hardest the longest.* We had thirty more minutes of unfinished business.

The second half belonged to our running backs: Dominic Rhodes and Joseph Addai. They thrashed that big, bad Bears defense for long gains and first downs. Though we couldn't ever get into the end zone, Vinatieri added a couple more field goals to make the score 22–14. As a defense, we continued to get the Bears offense off the field. In turn, we dominated a key stat—plays from scrimmage—with sixty-six plays for our offense compared to only twenty-eight for Chicago. We had the ball for sixteen more minutes than they did, a sign that they would fatigue quickly. We were winning the game physically and emotionally, but when their kicker, Robbie Gould, hit a field goal, we found ourselves again only up by one possession. The score stood 22–17. Despite outplaying them, the next big play would likely determine the outcome of the game.

The Bears were backed up in their own territory, but gained a valuable first down to extend their drive.

Bears' ball, first and ten at their own thirty-eight yard line; two receivers spread out to the left. Grossman drops to throw. Pump fakes. Throws a deep ball...Intercepted by Kelvin Hayden! Sprinting down the field he goes. He's at the fifty, forty-five, down to the forty, the thirty-five. He may score. Fifteen! Ten! Five! Touchdown Kelvin Haden!"

Kelvin hadn't even played during many of the games' snaps. Nick Harper had given us everything he had before he couldn't go anymore at the corner, and they'd put Kelvin in because he was more experienced than some of our younger players. Grossman and his receiver tried a double move, but Kelvin didn't bite on the fake. When the ball came toward him he went up, snagged it at his highest point, and started racing down field as soon as his feet touched the turf. He straddled the sideline as he ran, shaking one defender and then another. The rest of the defense provided him with a convoy as he drew near the end zone. The touchdown made the score 29–17, a two-possession game.

The Bears challenged the play to see if Kelvin had stepped out of bounds. He hadn't, but his toe had been only a hair from the line. When the referees came over the speaker to say that the challenge was denied—*The touchdown stands*—our sideline exploded. In celebration, we did our signature rain gesture, flipping money on Kelvin and symbolically making it "rain" money on him.

On the next series, Grossman tried to force in another throw, resulting in another interception, this time by Bob Sanders. This sealed the game to the point that we drenched Coach Dungy with a Gatorade bath. He had done it. We had done it. We were Super Bowl Champs!

Later, as the confetti exploded overhead, raining down on us alongside the real raindrops that hadn't stopped falling all game, I hugged my teammates. We hoisted Coach Dungy on our shoulders, and soon after, my family came onto the field from the stands. I wanted them there for this moment. My agents Mike and Justin joined us, alongside my big cousin Lew, my brothers and sister, and my fiancé. We all relished the moment, not saying much, just looking around at the chaos of activity and excitement. At one point, Cato and I met up, both smiled, and shared a brief moment.

"All that work paid off, man," he said. "How does it feel?"

"It was all worth it. Paid off big time."

As the NFL folks brought out the trophy, we all lined up and rubbed it as it went to the top of the podium. Though Peyton won the MVP trophy, in a game this big there are lots of people who play invaluable roles. Our two running backs, Bob Sanders, Robert Mathis, Kelvin Hayden…all of these guys were MVPs as well. As I stood there with my teammates, it felt almost as if time stood still. I could have stayed in that moment forever.

Unfortunately, the media called. We were escorted off the field, some folks stopping to answer questions with reporters, and made our way into the locker room, where we posed with the Lombardi trophy and turned the celebration up a notch.

When I arrived at my locker, Cato was holding court. Somehow he got a hold of a microphone, and he came to me for an interview.

"Gary Brackett, how you doing today?"

"Man, I feel like a champion."

"You are a champion."

"I am a champion. That's right."

"At Rutgers, you won a combined…in four years you won about…"

"I'd rather not talk about that right now. I just want to talk about the present. You know, they said we were too small. They said we couldn't tackle. Said our defense couldn't win a championship. Man, they said a lot of things. They just counted us out."

"And what happened then?"

"We didn't believe them. We listened to one voice—Coach Dungy. We got it done. Picked up our bootstraps."

"Bootstraps."

"I picked up your bootstraps."

Cato laughed, "I didn't know you played football with bootstraps."

"Picked up our cleats then."

The interviews continued from there. The gist of the matter was that we were not in position to celebrate however pleased we were. We were having fun. Coach Dungy stood up to address us all together.

"I am so proud of you guys."

The feeling was mutual. We were proud to be associated with this coach, this team, this organization. Coach Dungy then called us up and told us how proud he was of us but the feeling was likewise. He would tell us what time we were leaving in the morning and that we would finish the game the same way we had always started it, with the Lord's Prayer:

> *Our Father, which art in heaven,*
> *hallowed be thy name.*
> *Thy Kingdom come,*
> *thy will be done,*
> *on earth as it is in heaven*
> *Give us this day our daily bread.*
> *And forgive us our trespasses,*
> *as we forgive them that trespass against us.*
> *And lead us not into temptation,*
> *but deliver us from evil.*
> *For thine is the kingdom,*
> *the power, and the glory,*
> *for ever and ever.*
> *Amen.*

The morning after that Super Bowl came early. I had agreed to an appearance on a local morning show that had reporters in Miami, earning myself a 7:00 a.m. start to the day after a late night. Bright idea. I was exhausted, but had committed and didn't want to break my word. When the alarm sounded, I rolled my legs over the side of the bed to experienced a rude surprise: I still had to put those pants on one leg at a time. The water as I washed my face didn't feel particularly fresher...just water.

Sometimes in life we get so caught up in reaching a particular pinnacle that we don't think much about what we'll do when we get there. We often don't realize that the work to sustain that success will be just as demanding. As the Super Bowl champs, the next year we were going to face stiff competition from all of our opponents. We'd have the bull's eye on our chest.

Any time I start gearing up for new challenges I think about where I've been, the various journeys that have brought me to where I am today. I've gone from a high school all-state player who had to walk on to my college team, where I eventually earned a scholarship and went on to be a two-time MVP of my team. I graduated college, perhaps the most special achievement of all, and was signed as a free agent in the NFL. I made an NFL team, not just any team, but a really great team. Through all this, now I am a starter on the Super Bowl Champion Indianapolis Colts. God is extremely good. It just goes to show in life it doesn't matter where you start but where you finish.

After the interview, I went back to my room and got my things ready to get on the bus to go back to Indianapolis. We had won and were sure that our fans back home wanted to greet us as World Champs. The city scheduled a parade to take place when we arrived, the parade culminating at the RCA Dome. Just one thing, though, parades don't work so well in Indy during February. Crowds can withstand a lot to show their affection, but minus five degrees is a bit much to ask. Nevertheless, we rode on some makeshift trailers through the streets of our city toward the RCA Dome with speakers blaring "We Are the Champions."

We came around the corner and turned onto Capitol Street to see the white top of the RCA Dome gleaming in the cold. The crowd swelled as we neared the gates, and when we came into RCA we experienced full sensory overload. First of all, we were literally coming in out of the cold, and were excited for some warmth after that Indiana winter air.

But that didn't compare with the noise. Our fans were louder than I ever heard them before. At the time, the dome was one of the loudest stadiums in the NFL, and it was alleged by some of our opponents that we were pumping sound to distract them. If those opponents had been there on that day, they would have heard decibel levels foreign even to me. As the franchise had grown, our fans grew as supporters each and every year and became better and better at expressing their love for the Colts.

After a couple guys spoke, the defense went to the microphone and made our message short and simple: "Repeat! Repeat!"

We screamed this again and again, but even in the midst of our excitement I thought to myself, if only it were that easy. For I couldn't forget that during a sixteen-month span, I lost my father, mother, and brother.

I may have been a champion in sporting life, but the globe seemed to keep right on spinning, bringing with it a mixture of professional and personal developments. The next year the Colts picked up right where we left off. We started the season 13–2 and continued to excel as one of the best teams in the NFL.

In that early success, my mood was dampened by one thing: I missed my old friend Cato, who had signed with the Tampa Bay Buccaneers during the off-season. My routines changed without him. I no longer had a carpool partner and someone to chat with on rides to and from work. Nonetheless, the NFL is a business, and business for the Colts that year was good until we ended up losing early in the playoffs to the San Diego Chargers. Sometimes the fates just don't line up.

That season was one of my best as a professional. I ended up with 119 tackles and four interceptions, and hoped that those numbers would be enough to propel me into the Pro Bowl for the first time. After our team success, I viewed that personal accolade as another step in my career. The Pro Bowl invitation didn't happen, a fact I attributed as much to fan favorites as reality. But after such a year I did start thinking about renegotiating my contract.

The contract I had signed two years prior was chump change in comparison to the contracts of my peers. My total compensation equaled what many other players of my caliber received as a signing bonus. Since my stats suggested that I was one of the better linebackers in the league, I figured that it was time the numbers on my checks aligned more closely with the facts on the field.

In the wake of the Pro Bowl snub, and as my doubts about my long-term contract grew, I began to get more and more frustrated. I moped around the house feeling sorry for myself for weeks. I wondered why, after all the effort I had expended over the years, results had not come. A symbol of my past finally snapped me out of that self-pity. As I was heading to the kitchen to get another bad microwave dinner from the freezer, for some reason my eyes lingered a bit on a framed poem my mom had given me years earlier. The poem is titled "Footprints," and it talks about, when life is toughest, God actually stops walking beside us. At times He even carries us when we are too weak to go forward on our own.

FOOTPRINTS

One night I had a dream--
I dreamed I was walking along the beach with the Lord
and across the sky flashed scenes from my life.
For each scene I noticed two sets of footprints,
one belonged to me and the other to the Lord.
When the last scene of my life flashed before me,
I looked back at the footprints in the sand.
I noticed that many times along the path of my life,
there was only one set of footprints.
I also noticed that it happened at the very lowest
and saddest times in my life.
This really bothered me and I questioned the Lord about it.
"Lord, you said that once I decided to follow you,
you would walk with me all the way,
but I have noticed that during the most troublesome times in my life
there is only one set of footprints.

"I don't understand why in times when I needed you most,
you should leave me."
The Lord replied, "My precious, precious child,
I love you and I would never, never leave you
during your times of trial and suffering.
"When you saw only one set of footprints,
it was then that I carried you."
– Mary Stevenson

As I thought of that message, and the optimism my mom had instilled in me, that old self-pity dissolved. What is for me, I said to myself, is for me. What comes will come. But I've got to put my faith in God and stop feeling sorry for myself.

This new attitude was helped by developments off the field. I had long promised myself that I would remain romantically uncommitted until my playing days were over. But things have a way of changing. Change came to me in the form of Ragan. She was a local girl from Indianapolis who I met during my rookie season. At the time, she had just moved back home after graduating from Brown University in Providence, Rhode Island. She was studying for the MCAT, but I'd pry a date from her on occasion. First, though, I had to pry from her a phone number. Since she was busy with studying, and I had a variety of irons on the fire, we didn't really grow serious for a while.

After a trip to Nashville for surgery to repair my injured hip, things with Ragan began in earnest. I was on crutches in recovery and she came to visit. When she saw me she joked with me some, "Well, look at the big, tough football player on his crutches."

"Yeah, I am not going to win a foot race anytime soon, huh?"

"What have you been eating?" she asked me.

"Mostly Lean Cuisine meals. I don't want to put on too much weight while I'm away from working out."

Ragan said, "Those can't be too tasty."

"Yeah," I responded, "I can understand why people lose weight on them. I can barely finish the things they are so bad."

She offered to do a bit of shopping and cooking for me, which was probably the moment when our future went from possibility to probability. As my mom said, "Face powder can get a man, but baking powder keeps him."

Our relationship accelerated after that one evening, and my rehab progressed nicely, too. The next football season did not start out as well. We were accustomed to fast starts and lots of wins early. The beginning of 2008 did not offer anything quickly except for difficulties. We lost our first game to the Bears, a portent of struggles to come. The turn in our play came, probably, in Texas. I played a key role, and still see my name pop up on YouTube for running a fumble back for a touchdown. We ended up winning that game with a great comeback, but things eventually ended poorly for the Colts and me. I broke my fibula and spent the last few games of the season on the sidelines, so I wasn't on the field when the Colts once again bowed out of the playoffs early, courtesy once again of the San Diego Chargers.

In summary, after our Super Bowl victory, we had suffered two early post-season losses. We needed to turn things around. Though developments were mostly disappointing on the field, my personal life brought changes that were more positive.

My relationship with Ragan took on a new level of meaningful connection in the off-season. We found out that Ragan was pregnant. Although the surprise announcement meant some sudden changes, we prepared to raise a child together. With the doctor visits and planning, we began to spend even more time together. In the face of this new responsibility, our bond grew stronger. Despite my warnings—*don't let yourself fall for someone before your career is over*—sometimes a heart has different plans. As I watched her gracefully navigate carrying a child, attending med school, and counseling me about my career path, I knew without question that she was the one I wanted to spend the rest of my life with. I asked Ragan to marry me, and she said yes.

They say that, in life, when it rains it pours. Well, sometimes we invite the weather. While Ragan and I planned on the coming child, I unwittingly added another element to consider. My nephews and nieces often came to visit me in the off-season. For Greg's children especially, I try to be available and serve as a sort of role model. During that off-season following the 2008 season, my nephew Gregory came to visit. He and I had a great time together. We'd play games, go out for ice cream, all the stuff that kids like to do. I tried to, when I wasn't working out, give him my full attention. Our bond developed, and over time he began to express his affection for me with questions asking for more: "Gary, can I come live with you?"

When it wasn't that, he referenced his lack of a father figure: "Can you be my dad?"

I knew his mom had her hands full back home, so at some point I responded to his pleas with, "I'll talk to your Mom."

That conversation got the ball rolling. It rolled all the way to Gregory moving from New Jersey to Indianapolis to live with us. As the Colts went through two strong seasons and two disappointing post-seasons, I got engaged, began planning on a baby's arrival, and adopted my nephew. It was a busy time to say the least! Ragan accepted all of these developments with her trademark calm and composure.

Fortunately, on the field, the season of 2009 started out differently. After 2008, Coach Dungy retired, and Coach Jim Caldwell took the helm. Our defense welcomed some of the changes that Caldwell's arrival ushered in, specifically in the form of our new coordinator, Larry Coyer. In Coach Coyer's system, we blitzed more and played a style that was generally more aggressive. The results were good. We had a strong early season record and even flirted with perfection once again, running our record to 14–0 before losing to the Jets. Coach Caldwell's decision to rest the starters late in the season in that game against the Jets brought him some criticism, but also underlined his overarching goal. He wanted to win a championship, whether or not we won all of our regular season games. Though we lost our perfect record to the Jets late in the season, we eventually beat them in the AFC Championship to punch our tickets back to the Super Bowl.

Our opponent this time was the New Orleans Saints, but the site of the game was the same. We'd be heading back to Miami! The lead-up to the game prompted a bit less reflection from my end. After all, I'd been in the very same rooms and in front of the very same podiums before. Questions focused less in that second game on my history as a walk-on than on my future. Would I be with the Colts next season? Did I have any thoughts on the upcoming contract negotiations? Where did I want to be next season? I had no intention of answering those questions. Doing so would undermine any leverage I had, but I wanted badly to be in Indianapolis. I had a fiancé who very much wanted the same thing.

The Saints were a great team with America rooting for them. After Katrina in 2005, New Orleans was still in recovery mode four years later. Parts of the city were still abandoned, many because rebuilding and resettlement had been slower than hoped. So, not only we were playing a good football team, but we were also playing the sentimental pick for many fans across the country. When I walked onto the field for that game, I was a bit less distracted. I'd need all the focus I could muster. Though the Saints had my respect, I had no intention of lying down or giving in to sentiment.

The game was tight in the first half. We scored the first ten points, and went into the locker rooms for halftime with a lead. Coming out of halftime, Sean Peyton and his Saints team executed perfectly what will surely go down as one of the gutsiest calls in Super Bowl history. They came out and on-side kicked to start the half. Nobody does that! After the Saints recovered, the game was pretty much all New Orleans. They went on to beat us 31–17.

As good as it felt two years prior to hoist the Lombardi trophy, it felt twice as bad to lose it. I personally had a good game, ending up with a game-high thirteen tackles along with a stop on fourth down that prevented a score in the first half.

But those personal achievements were secondary, and this loss felt dramatic and heartbreaking. What could we have done differently? We had started the season with fourteen straight wins and now were totally devastated. Now we had even more work to do to get another victory on this biggest of stages. We needed to remember not to lose the lesson in this loss.

As the defeat slowly grew more and more real to me over the next couple days, I began to think more clearly about my future. This could have been my last game as a Colt. Obviously, I felt sad about the possibility of that relationship ending. My agent was sure that I had put myself on the map going into the off-season, especially after an extremely strong post-season. As things developed, many football people came to consider me the second hottest middle linebacker free agent after Karlos Dansby of the Cardinals.

Free agency during the off-season wasn't the only thing that I was worried about. Ragan and I had scheduled our wedding for that summer. We had all the planning for that, though I tried as much as possible to stay out of it. In addition to those two levels of stress, I worried about my nephew Greg. Since he'd moved in with us, he was struggling with living so far away from his mother and his sisters. His worries compounded my own, and these various elements of stress plagued me daily. If I wasn't worried about one thing, I was worried about another. The contract process added fuel to the fire.

After the Super Bowl, the Colts called my agent to start dialogue about new contract numbers. As with most contracts, at the beginning it felt like both parties were hopelessly far from each other. Both try to maximize perceived advantages and positions of strength. The Colts knew that I had set roots in Indianapolis, and they knew that for an athlete like me, playing for a well-run organization that won consistently was very important. The team was successful—we had won 115 games in the last decade, the most of any team in the NFL during that time period.

My bargaining position, the fact that I was a captain and had played a part in so many victories, enhanced my position. Other teams would pay a premium for that sort of experience. A proven winner is no small thing in the locker room, on the practice field, and in game situations.

My agents laid out essentially two choices for this process: try to negotiate solely with the Colts, or go out and entertain offers from other teams. The prospect of other offers and a recruiting process was alluring.

Remember, I'd never really been recruited. It would feel nice to have teams pursue me like that. I was tempted by that process, but weighed that temptation against the sense of loyalty I'd developed toward the Colts. They had been so good to me through so many personal tragedies. They were like family. In the end, I decided to hammer something out with the Colts and focus on negotiations with only one team.

The class of the Colts played an essential role in the way those negotiations went. In my mind, the organization is second to none. Whereas other owners view their players as disposable cattle in the barn of their team, the Colts' owner, Mr. Irsay, views players as business partners and employees worthy of respect. He respects every player on his team. Not only does he talk respectfully to the franchise player, he also looks out for the rookie free agent that was just picked up last week.

This all played a huge role in my decision to stay. So many players make decisions to leave for a payday in some other locale. They perhaps think that with that money, the grass will be greener elsewhere. But, as my personal trainer, Greg Moore, says, "The grass is only as green as you water it."

My decision to bargain only with the Colts was hardly the end of the process. In the NFL, teams face certain deadlines for signing free agents. After that prescribed date, things get a good bit more difficult with the negotiations. As we approached the beginning of the free agency period, I began to worry about what would happen if we didn't agree to terms in time. The contract discussions were stalling a bit, and I fretted about whether or not I'd made the right decision to focus singularly on the Colts. But just a couple hours into the first day of free agency, right after 12:00, I signed a five-year deal with the team I'd come up with. The signing bonus alone on this new contract was more money than I'd made in my first seven years in the league. I felt like all the hard work over the years had been validated. To be paid as one of the best middle linebackers in the NFL symbolized for me long-term professional success.

Only one person was more excited about the new contract than I was; Ragan was absolutely ecstatic. The deal meant that we wouldn't have to move and that she could continue at medical school without interruptions. We immediately started looking for a new house. Nothing fit the bill precisely, so we decided to build something in which we could be comfortable for the long term. In some of my business deals, I'd met a builder named Kenneth Taylor. He'd become a great friend, and I trusted him absolutely to build our dream home.

With the home planning process and the wedding details, July arrived like a flash. We enjoyed a wedding that was lots of fun and also elegant. The day of the ceremony, I looked around at all of my family and friends in one place together. The only other time that ever happens is for funerals, and I'd experienced my share of those. It was good to see all of those same people on a much happier occasion. Uncles and siblings commented on how much pain we'd come through to reach this happier day.

We lit candles for all of our loved ones, particularly my parents, Greg, and Ragan's dad. Memories of those loved ones, and our sorrow that those now gone could not be in that moment to share it, were alleviated somewhat by all the new family members we were adding to our circle with this union. We drank champagne and toasted to new beginnings. We did not forget from whence we'd come: From a walk-on at Rutgers to a well-paid professional football player. From someone used to long-distance relationships to marriage. From son to father. Yet, we knew then that our journey was in many ways just beginning.

As a professional athlete, I dwell daily in sports metaphors and analogies. Coaches tell us stories of former teams and victories they've won through working together. Sports writers make comparisons of one comeback to another. The hope is that for athletes, those sports stories can inspire some similar level of achievement or determination in our athletic careers.

But sports extend beyond themselves. The lessons they teach are not limited to the boundary lines of the playing field—those lessons are relevant in the world. I think frequently about the greater sports moments of our time, the ones that represent sports at their best, creating in my mind a sort of Mt. Rushmore of sports' stories. Was the greatest achievement the night Michael Jordan went for sixty-three points in Madison Square Garden against the Knicks? Was it when Reggie Jackson hit three home runs for the Yankees in a single World Series game? Was it when sports pushed society toward broader change, like when Jackie Robinson silently and graciously broke the color barrier of baseball, or when Coach Dungy became the first African American coach to win a Super Bowl?

In my mind, those are all stories of true greatness. But the pinnacle of my Mt. Rushmore, the story that speaks most directly to me in my own life, is one of a horse: Secretariat. This horse ran faster than any horse ever had or has since. But one particular aspect of Secretariat's performance is symbolic for me of the way I want to live my life. Though there are events year-round, the world of horse racing leads annually to three specific races that together form the Triple Crown.

The first race of the Triple Crown is the Kentucky Derby. The track is one-and-a-quarter miles long, and Secretariat spanned that distance in one minute, fifty-nine seconds. The sheer speed is astounding, and to this day has not been equaled, but Secretariat's place on my Mount Rushmore of sports stories isn't based solely on the fact that he ran fast. Races are broken down in quarter-mile increments, and the speed of each quarter is compared to the earlier quarters. Secretariat did something amazing in Louisville, Kentucky, that day. He accelerated the entire race.

Nor did he stop in Kentucky. He won the second race of the Triple Crown, the Preakness, in fine form a few weeks later. Finally, the *coup de grace*, Secretariat blew away the field for the last of the three Triple Crown races, the Belmont Stakes, by going thirty-three lengths faster than any other horse. The announcer, when you go back and listen to the audio, dwells repeatedly on one fact during the last part of the race: "Secretariat is still widening his lead. Still widening."

This is what I think we must strive for in our own lives. We must accelerate the entire length of our days. If we live to be one hundred years old, every quarter ought to be better than the ones before. The best is always yet to come. We might not all be physically capable of outpacing everyone else. But we are all capable of getting stronger as we go along.

And how do we do that? I believe that we must live our lives like that Rutgers coach told me to play, like the score is tied at zero and we only have one shot to impress. What you are doing at any moment, do to the best of your ability. We must never limit ourselves to the lower bar right in front of us. We must reach higher than we think possible to the level that seems out of our reach. We must refuse to be satisfied at easy success. If you can only do this, whatever tests come at you, you'll overcome them and have added material for your own future testimony!

ABOUT THE AUTHOR

GARY BRACKETT was a star football player at Glassboro High School and later at Rutgers University where he was named defensive captain and won the team's defensive MVP honors. Gary Brackett was signed by the Indianapolis Colts as an undrafted free agent; three years later, he was named defensive captain of the Colts and played a key role in their Super Bowl XLI win over the Chicago Bears.

Gary and his wife, Ragan, live in Indianapolis with their two beautiful children.